MATT HARTLEY

Matt Hartley grew up in the ⎯⎯⎯ ... and studied Drama at the University of Hull. Matt's first play *Sixty Five Mile*s won a Bruntwood Award in the inaugural Bruntwood Competition and was produced by Paines Plough/Hull Truck. Other theatre includes *Here I Belong* (Pentabus Theatre Company); *Myth*, co-written with Kirsty Housley (RSC); *Deposit* (Hampstead Theatre); *Horizon* (National Theatre Connections); *Microcosm* (Soho Theatre); *The Bee* (Edinburgh Festival); *Punch* (Hampstead Theatre/Heat and Light Company); *Epic* and *Trolls* (Theatre503). Radio includes *Tracks*, *The Pursuit* and *Final Call* (Radio 4). Matt is currently writing new plays for Radio 4, Hampstead Theatre, Leeds Playhouse and the Sherman Theatre.

Matt Hartley

# EYAM

NICK HERN BOOKS
London
www.nickhernbooks.co.uk

**A Nick Hern Book**

*Eyam* first published in Great Britain as a paperback original in 2018 by Nick Hern Books Limited, The Glasshouse, 49a Goldhawk Road, London W12 8QP

*Eyam* copyright © 2018 Matt Hartley

Matt Hartley has asserted his right to be identified as the author of this work

Cover image: Superunion

Designed and typeset by Nick Hern Books, London
Printed in the UK by Mimeo Ltd, Huntingdon, Cambridgeshire PE29 6XX

A CIP catalogue record for this book is available from the British Library

ISBN 978 1 84842 772 3

*Eyam* was first performed at Shakespeare's Globe, London, on 15 September 2018, with the following cast:

| | |
|---|---|
| MR THOMAS STANLEY | Annette Badland |
| ELIZABETH HANCOCK/<br>   ELIZABETH SHELDON | Zora Bishop |
| PHILIP SHELDON/<br>   JOHN WILSON | Adrian Bower |
| KATHERINE MOMPESSON | Priyanga Burford |
| REV. SHORELAND ADAMS/<br>   JOHN HANCOCK | John Paul Connolly |
| REV. WILLIAM MOMPESSON | Sam Crane |
| ELIZABETH SYDALL/<br>   MARY TALBOT | Becci Gemmell |
| JOHN SYDALL | Will Keen |
| EMMOTT SYDALL | Norah Lopez-Holden |
| EDWARD COOPER/<br>   ROWLAND TORRE | Luke MacGregor |
| FRANCIS BOCKINGE/<br>   GEORGE VICCARS | Jordan Metcalfe |
| UNWIN | Oliver Ryan |
| MARY COOPER | Sirine Saba |
| MARSHALL HOWE | Howard Ward |
| HARRIET STUBBS | Rose Wardlaw |

| | |
|---|---|
| *Director* | Adele Thomas |
| *Designer* | Hannah Clark |
| *Composer* | Orlando Gough |
| *Choreographer* | Emma Woods |
| *Assistant Director* | Hila Ben-Ari |
| *Fight Director* | Kevin McCurdy |
| *Head of Casting* | Karishma Balani |

## Character Biographies

### REVEREND WILLIAM MOMPESSON

Oxbridge-educated, Royalist, appointment by Sir Saville. Previously posted in a small village close to Scarborough. Youthful and ambitious, he is prone to three words when one would do. He is a strong public speaker when talking to the right crowd. He has never been in a fight or held a shovel.

### KATHERINE MOMPESSON

Bright and sharp-witted, she arrives in Eyam after a period of illness. Most likely what we now call post-natal depression. She is a few years older than William and this often proves to be valuable in her ability to see the world and its people more clearly. She is desperate for a fresh start. Both her and William are more free-spirited in their services and she has long encouraged the act of singing. Not afraid to get her hands dirty.

### MR THOMAS STANLEY

In today's terms he is a Puritan. Long-standing religious leader of Eyam who was exiled when the act of uniformity was passed. Beloved by as many of the villagers as he is feared. Unwavering faith but now destitute and widowed. He arrives a broken man.

### REVEREND SHORELAND ADAMS

Sir Saville's previous appointment. A bloated, corrupt man of the church who for years has plundered what little material wealth the church and parishioners of Eyam possessed.

### JOHN HANCOCK

A giant man of the land and natural leader. A free miner. He has a smallholding, upon which he mines for lead and farms livestock. He fought in the Civil War for the Parliamentarian cause. The Hancocks' neighbour is Mary Talbot, who is John's dearest friend.

## ELIZABETH HANCOCK

A woman of the land. Strong as an ox but exhausted from the hell that is her daily life of washing ore and maintaining a barren outcrop of land. She is ready for a change.

## MARY TALBOT

Fierce and proud, she has worked on the land all her life. She would be the first on the picket line and the last to walk away. She suffered at the hands of marauding soldiers during the Civil War.

## UNWIN

One of life's natural schemers and opportunists. Local poacher and trader of meat. Adept with a knife and acerbic wit. Would have fought in the war for whichever side was winning at the time. He is a terrible fighter but loves a scrap – after all, it's the taking part that counts.

## MARSHALL HOWE

Church sexton. Was a lead miner. Always hungry and late for his dinner. Finally and happily married late in life. Prone to helping himself to the property of those he buries, and handy with his fists.

## HARRIET STUBBS

Turns twelve during the play. She's wild and inquisitive. Raised by no one but smacked by all. As likely to be found kicking a dead cat as she is to sneak into your house and watch you sleep.

## MARY COOPER

A loudmouth self-opinionated Puritan, who is as adapt at hypocrisy as she is at suppressing her son, who she loves with all of her heart. Her house gives her the perfect vantage to be the community's most nosy neighbour, and boy does she make use of it. She is Francis Bockinge's sister-in-law and has recently relinquished her land to Sheldon. The money left from both of her deceased husbands' estates is running dry, which is why she is forced to rent out her room.

## EDWARD COOPER

A walking pair of eyes. He's nineteen but has the worldly knowledge of someone half his age. His father died in the mines and he has been wrapped in cotton wool ever since by his overbearing mother, who will do almost anything to keep him safe, even if that means quashing his spirit. When George Viccars arrives, his world explodes, and all the confusion he has often felt begins to make sense.

## GEORGE VICCARS

Early twenties. An itinerant tailor who is exceptional at his job. He is from a large northern town and is as easy in the company of wealthy clients as he is with those who have not a penny to their name. He truly knows who he is. As befitting a man who travels, his life has been hard and often wrought with danger, as he navigates the precarious highways of northern England.

## JOHN SYDALL

Once he was the village yob and drunk who was a tenacious miner, but one morning, whilst lying in a pile of his own excrement, he saw the light of God. Stanley took him in and taught him to read. Unfortunately in Stanley's absence nobody has been able to curb Sydall's natural ferociousness and anger. He has stopped working in order to share the word of God as loudly and with as much vengeance as the good Lord has bestowed upon him.

## ELIZABETH SYDALL

Long-suffering wife and devoted mother. She is employed by Sheldon as a maid, and since her husband stopped working, this has been the family's sole source of income. Every inch of her being is in love with John Wilson and in any other lifetime she may have been the person her daughter Emmott is.

## EMMOTT SYDALL

The epicentre of any party. Emmott may end up starting a revolution. She was the apple of her father's eye until she hit puberty and started to question the world. Having watched her mother live in fear, it is an emotion she has promised to never let dictate her own life. Rowland is the roots to her tree.

## ROWLAND TORRE

Solid muscle. He would walk through a wall rather than step over it. He is not a man prone to sentiment so love is a baffling but completely genuine experience for him.

## JOHN WILSON

Elizabeth Sydall was his childhood sweetheart but their relationship was never able to be made true as he was enlisted to fight in the war. He was presumed dead in the war. He survived horrific wounds and after many years of trekking finally found his way home, only to find Elizabeth had married John Sydall. Since his return he has turned down potential suitors and remains unmarried. He now works back in the mines and will do anything in his power to protect the woman he loves.

## FRANCIS BOCKINGE

Injured by an accident working in the mines, Francis's stutter has become more pronounced since he has been forced to work for Sheldon. His wife Jude was the last person Howe buried before the play starts, and her loss weighs heavily upon him. A deeply selfless man, he places great faith in Stanley who has always taken care of him. Edward Cooper's uncle.

## PHILIP SHELDON

A bastard who revels in being a complete arsehole. He once was a free miner, with the most productive piece of land. During the Civil War he started selling lead to rivaling causes and has since become the wealthiest man in the village. He now occupies the largest house in the village and has bought out the majority of the villagers' land, with only two pieces remaining (Hancock and Talbot), which will ensure his complete control of the village and the wealth it contains. He hates the chattering classes but desperately longs to be accepted by them.

## ELIZABETH SHELDON

From the neighbouring village of Tideswell. She is the local beauty who Sheldon has effectively bought after the death of her beloved first husband's death. She is desperately lonely and trapped in the cage that Sheldon has created for her. Much younger than her husband.

## Acknowledgements

*Eyam* is a story that I have wanted to tell since I was eight years old. I would like to thank the entire team at the Globe that have crafted and built this show and brought that ambition to life.

Dr Will Tosh, Jennifer Edwards and the wonderful team of researchers who have been invaluable. The team and staff at Eyam museum and church: thank you for your generosity and enthusiasm. Andy Wood for writing a book that gave me the confidence to commit to the wild west. All those that I grew up with who have provided the springboard into this world.

Ben Addis, Paul Copley, Shaun Dooley, Laura Elsworthy, David Hartley, Simon Harrison, John Heffernan, Rebecca Humphries, Paul Kaye, Richard Lumsden, Laura Morgan, Jenny Rainsford, Felix Scott and Susie Trayling for being integral in giving these characters voices. Dave Bond, Heather Davies and the students at RWCMD for being such willing guinea pigs.

Karishma Balani, Pippa Hill, Jessica Lusk, Severine Magois, Carole Moorcraft, Lisa Spirling and the team at Nick Hern Books. Jennifer Thomas and Giles Smart for getting this over the line.

Rebecca Askew, Jeremy Avis, Hila Ben-Ari, Lauren Burns, Sarah Case, Ian Farmery, Kevin McCurdy and Amy Slater for all your commitment to the Eyam cause.

Annette Badland, Zora Bishop, Adrian Bower, Priyanga Burford, Sam Crane, John Paul Connolly, Becci Gemmell, Will Keen, Norah Lopez-Holden, Luke MacGregor, Jordan Metcalfe, Oliver Ryan, Sirine Saba, Howard Ward and Rose Wardlaw for bringing this story to life so vividly.

Hannah Clark, Orlando Gough and Emma Woods: true collaborators who gave such brilliant notes and then created such a vivid language to tell Eyam's story.

I will forever be in awe and debt to Michelle Terry whose unwavering belief and support is a gift that I wish upon every writer.

Adele Thomas: without your dedication, friendship, wisdom and vision this play wouldn't exist. Dioch cariad.

My parents and brother, for bringing Eyam into my life and putting up with me when it took over.

And of course my wife and daughter, my brilliant little community.

*M.H.*

*For Eden and Helen x*

**Author's Note**

This play is inspired by real events, it is not intended to be read as fact.

Dancing and singing is a vital part of Eyam's story. At the end of Part One the hymn sung by the villagers is: 'And Am I Born To Die' by Charles Wesley. The same hymn is repeated during Scene Forty. Although Wesley was born post the story it is believed this song was created by being inspired by his visit to Eyam. Throughout the script a mention to song is repeatedly made: this is original music created by Orlando Gough. Any production should look to create their own sound that amplifies the experience in these sections.

Any production should embrace the crows' theatricality. They are the size of the villagers.

In Scene Two, William initially mispronounces Eyam as 'I am'.

## Characters

REVEREND SHORELAND ADAMS
PHILIP SHELDON
REVEREND WILLIAM MOMPESSON
KATHERINE MOMPESSON
MARSHALL HOWE
HARRIET STUBBS
EDWARD COOPER
MARY COOPER
UNWIN
ELIZABETH HANCOCK
JOHN HANCOCK
FRANCIS BOCKINGE
MARY TALBOT
JOHN SYDALL
ELIZABETH SYDALL
JOHN WILSON
GEORGE VICCARS
ELIZABETH SHELDON
MR THOMAS STANLEY
EMMOTT SYDALL
ROWLAND TORRE

*The play is set in the village of Eyam, Derbyshire, between the years 1665 and 1666.*

## Note on Text

*A forward slash (/) indicates continued speech.*

*This text went to press before the end of rehearsals and so may differ slightly from the play as performed.*

## PART ONE

**1.**

*Eyam. 1665. Dawn. Church grounds.* REVEREND
SHORELAND ADAMS *hurries through the churchyard. The
bell rings. 5 a.m. Each chime speeds* ADAMS. *Shadows step
forth from the dark. They block his path.*

ADAMS. Stand back, stand back! I shall strike thee down!

*A figure grabs him.*

Release me, immediate!

*A hooded figure* (PHILIP SHELDON) *steps forth.* ADAMS
*recognises his shape.*

Wait. Pray wait…

SHELDON. String him up for all to see.

ADAMS.…I beg you. No…

*The figures drag* ADAMS *onto the floor. They tie a rope
round him, drag him through the mud towards a tree.*

I am a man of God. This will not go unpunished. Hear you
all, I am a servant of the Lord our Saviour!

SHELDON *gestures for them to hoist* ADAMS. *They follow
his instruction.*

SHELDON. Make yer peace, Adams.

ADAMS *dangles, his feet just remaining upon the floor.*

ADAMS. May you burn in hell.

SHELDON. Hoist him high.

ADAMS *is hoisted high. He dangles… the lynchers watch.*

God, whoever yer send next, let this be their greeting.

Welcome to Eyam.

*The* VILLAGERS *dance. Wild, aggressive. Their battle cry.*

**2.**

*Weeks later.*

*Eyam Church.*

REVEREND WILLIAM MOMPESSON *and*
KATHERINE MOMPESSON.

WILLIAM. Where has Sir Saville sent us?
  *Eyam,* a place no map will ever know.
  Lord, have I not served thee loyally?
  What wrong have I done to warrant this?

KATHERINE. Eyam.

WILLIAM. What?

KATHERINE. Locals pronounce it 'Eeeeam'.

WILLIAM. Eeeeem.

KATHERINE. There is an 'a' in there, William.

WILLIAM. EYAAAAM. Look at this church. Look above,
  Katherine. The sky! I can see the sky such is the hole in the
  roof. The floor, this wood, rotten. Squalor. Such utter disrepair.

KATHERINE. Enough of this self-pity, this wounded pride,
  William. No, Sir Saville has not sent us to a market town in
  a wholesome Midland shire, but he is not a man to appoint
  without reason.

WILLIAM. I only wish to serve God, to be a vessel for his
  words. To stand before a fine congregation, where words
  reach many not few. Yet instead here we stand: in
  insignificance. As what is this place, a populate no more than
  three hundred, what possible can be achieved?

*Crows cry.*

Crows! It even has roosting crows!!

KATHERINE. Crows. It is a sign!

WILLIAM. To flee.

KATHERINE. No. William, I have dreamt of them. Of this, the
  crows, so vividly.

WILLIAM. If crows haunt dreams it is a warning, Katherine. Not a sign to set up camp.

KATHERINE. No. I was not haunted. I have felt fear in dreams before. But never with these. It was as if they provided comfort. Peace.

WILLIAM. I shall send for the children immediate in that case.

KATHERINE. I can hear the mockery in your tone, but I beg you do. Not a moment passes where I do not feel the weight of their absence. Here. Eyam. This is God's plan. What form that takes I do not know. But is what he wishes. William, it is. I know it.

WILLIAM. Katherine, your passion is enough to make me question logic. Yet the children shall remain where they are. This place we know nothing of it yet.

KATHERINE. You cannot even say its name.

WILLIAM. Eyam.

KATHERINE. Hear that, you are a local already.

MARSHALL HOWE *enters*.

HOWE. Church's closed.

KATHERINE. The doors were open.

HOWE. Shouldn't be.

KATHERINE. Are you Marshall Howe?

HOWE. I am.

KATHERINE. You are the sexton here.

HOWE. I know that.

WILLIAM. I am Reverend William Mompesson, this is my wife Katherine.

HOWE. Not local.

KATHERINE. That is true.

HOWE. Whatever this be: visit, pilgrimage, some oddity a don't wish comprehend, know there is a time f'it: daytime. In short, out. Yer make me late for me dinner.

WILLIAM. He does not know who we are.

HOWE. A warning, it has been known for me to kick a man two foot through them doors for less than what you do now.

KATHERINE. Not the faintest idea. Mr Howe, William is your new reverend.

HOWE. No, he in't.

KATHERINE. Yes, he is.

HOWE. Sir Saville's appointment?

WILLIAM. Yes.

HOWE. Right. Bloody hell. I knew nothing of yer arrival.

KATHERINE. Not even our names?

HOWE. Nowt.

WILLIAM. Sir Saville sent letters, did they not arrive?

HOWE. If they did their news were never spread. If I were you I'd take this as golden opportunity, no one will be the wiser if yer turn back. I never saw yer.

KATHERINE. That will not be happening.

HOWE. Never forget I gave yer t'chance.

WILLIAM. Still wish to kick me through the door?

HOWE. Is me dinner to get cold?

WILLIAM. For tonight the locking will be our domain.

KATHERINE. Mr Howe, henceforth, I hope we will have no cause for quarrel.

HOWE. I dig graves where yer tell me then put dead people in 'em. Need be nowt more complicated than that.

*Something catches* HOWE's *eye.*

Oi! Oi, you!! I warned yer of this. Come out of there. Harriet!

HARRIET STUBBS *appears.*

Were yer sniffing round graves again?

HARRIET. I were hunting for rats.

HOWE. That's a lie. That's a finger in your hand.

HARRIET. Mrs Bockinge's. She used to poke me with it. Dead bony.

HOWE. Put it back.

HARRIET. She doesn't need it any more. Is he the new reverend?

HOWE. Yes.

HARRIET. Are they going to hang yer?

WILLIAM. What?

HOWE. Ignore the girl. She's a ghoul. Put that finger back. Now.

HARRIET *goes. Just as* MARY COOPER *enters with her son* EDWARD COOPER.

MARY COOPER. HOWE??????!!!!!!!!

HOWE. Oh not Mary Cooper, now I'm never going to get back f'me food.

MARY COOPER. I knew something were going on, I knew it! A carriage parked outside, I knew something were going on! I said that, didn't I, Edward.

EDWARD. You did, Mother. You said –

MARY COOPER. Hush, Edward! Who are they then?!

HOWE. Mary Cooper, there is not a corner of this village your nose dun't stick in.

MARY COOPER. Knowledge is power, Marshall Howe, be good for yer to remember that, things I've seen you do.

HOWE. S'new reverend and his wife.

MARY COOPER. Oh hello. Welcome. I am Mary Cooper. This thing here is my only child, Edward.

EDWARD. Good day. That is a lovely dress.

MARY COOPER. Edward, don't be so rude. Embarrassing me.

KATHERINE. It is alright. No offence was taken.

MARY COOPER. No, it is not alright! This boy is always making a scene. Go sit over there.

So do yer speak?!

WILLIAM. I do, yes. Reverend William Mompesson. My wife Katherine.

MARY COOPER. Are yer Saville's man?

WILLIAM. I say God's man foremost.

EDWARD *and* KATHERINE. Amen.

MARY COOPER *and* HOWE. Amen.

WILLIAM. But yes, Sir Saville is my patron.

MARY COOPER. Where have yer come from?

KATHERINE. Scarborough. Yorkshire.

HOWE. Well, if yer can make a man pray there yer can make a man pray anywhere.

EDWARD. What are your services like?

KATHERINE. That is a good question.

MARY COOPER. No need to humour him. Quiet, Edward!

EDWARD. Do you sing hymns?

MARY COOPER. Edward, I said quiet!

WILLIAM. We do.

MARY COOPER. Well then, we shan't be attending, as all know singing is the devil's entry point!

HARRIET *enters with* UNWIN.

HARRIET. He's in here.

UNWIN. Howe, outside now!

HOWE. Why?

UNWIN. I don't fight in churches.

HOWE. I'm busy, Unwin.

UNWIN. Not too busy to slander me and my meat!

HOWE. Meat? Yer taken liberty with that word, Unwin. If Noah, God rest his soul –

EDWARD. Amen.

ALL. Amen.

HOWE. Were to walk animals you butcher onto the Ark, be but one breed upon that vessel. 'N' that be a pony. Knackered old mule at that. /

UNWIN. Lies.

HOWE. / The one that has miraculously disappeared from Merrick's field to be particular.

UNWIN. Even if it were true. D' yer hear any other have qualm on quality of meat I provide?

HOWE. Silence is ransom held because you know there is no other meat could be afford bought.

UNWIN. None care if what they thinks pork is pork, cow cow, and it is but pony because in their mind 'tis what they want it to be. /

HARRIET. I like eating rats!

HOWE. Hear, he admits to all I pronounce!

UNWIN. / Truth is, Howe, it is not to my meat yer should look for complaint, but yer own home – for why be it my concern if yer wife cooks all meat so it tastes same?!

HOWE *goes towards* UNWIN.

HOWE. Never mock my wife, never! She's the finest cook!

EDWARD. This is no place for fighting.

HOWE *strikes* UNWIN. UNWIN *falls to the ground.* HOWE *continues to strike him.*

Mother, they're fighting!

HARRIET. Oh go suckle on yer mother's tit, Cooper, or hush yer hole.

WILLIAM. In God's name, enough.

*But it's not.* KATHERINE *instead races over and tries to pull* HOWE *off. In doing so she indadvertedly allows* UNWIN *to get a punch in.*

KATHERINE. Enough. Stop –

HOWE. Get off me! Nowt t'do with yer.

MARY COOPER. Aye, leave them. Let the fire burn itself out.

*They watch as* HOWE *beats* UNWIN.

HARRIET. That's a good hiding.

ELIZABETH *and* JOHN HANCOCK *approach. They take in the scene. They have buckets full of water with them.*

JOHN HANCOCK. Enough.

HOWE. Insulted my wife, John.

JOHN HANCOCK. Enough.

HOWE *relents. He stands, calms. Offers his hand to* UNWIN. UNWIN *shrugs* HOWE*'s help aside.*

Take his hand.

UNWIN. A need no aid. A can stand by meself, John Hancock.

UNWIN *slowly get to his feet. Then begins to spit blood and bits of broken teeth out.*

JOHN HANCOCK. You're the new reverend.

WILLIAM. William and Katherine Mompesson.

JOHN HANCOCK. Welcome. First time in Derbyshire?

WILLIAM. It is.

JOHN HANCOCK. You'll get used to it.

ELIZABETH HANCOCK. Elizabeth and John Hancock.

HOWE. Want sense in Eyam, head to them.

ELIZABETH HANCOCK. Be a compliment in any other village.

FRANCIS BOCKINGE *enters, he is a broken soul, damaged goods.*

FRANCIS. G-good-good-good day, all.

JOHN HANCOCK. Come of yer own accord, Francis?

FRANCIS. Mr She-Sheldon se-sends me, John.

JOHN HANCOCK. It be Mr Hancock if yer come on his terms.

FRANCIS. I. Must re-relay mess-message for the new-new
rev-reverend and wi-wife.

KATHERINE. Hello.

FRANCIS. Francis Bock-Bockinge. Rev-Reverend, Mrs-Mrs-
Mom-Mom–

JOHN HANCOCK. Francis is Mr Sheldon's messenger.

MARY COOPER. As cruel a joke as could be made.

WILLIAM. Mr Sheldon?

ELIZABETH HANCOCK. That name is new to you?

KATHERINE. Everything is new to us.

FRANCIS. Mr-Mr-Mr- She-he wishes to in-invite yer – for
a – din-dinner. This evening.

KATHERINE. This evening?

FRANCIS. Yer-you… will attend?

KATHERINE. We shall. Where does he live?

*Everyone stares in disbelief.*

What? We don't even know our own lodgings let alone others'.

ELIZABETH HANCOCK. Have no problem finding Sheldon's,
even at night his house cast shadow over entire village.

JOHN HANCOCK. Better run back to him now, Francis.

FRANCIS. There is m-more. Unwin. Mr Shel–Shel – He says –
where – where the – fu-fu- is the –

UNWIN. I have the stag. He will get it. Soon as I finish my
business with Howe.

KATHERINE. I think your business done there.

UNWIN. Anything but.

JOHN HANCOCK. Home now, Unwin.

UNWIN. I go where I want, John Hancock, where I want. 'N'
I want here. So here yer go, Reverend. Missus. Know this:
I poach, forage on others' land, on occasion mis-sell meat, aye.
I'm no angel, but I shall make my own peace with God on that.
But, whilst my heart still beats, I'll not be judged by that man.
A man who sinks depths lower than I could ever plumb. /

HOWE. Silence is yer only friend here, Unwin.

UNWIN. / A steaming pile of horse's shite is all he is. Sexton!
Yer see to die in this parish not only yer spirit that departs
but all yer worldly possessions not long after. He robs from
the dead!

HARRIET. Do yer? /

HOWE. Will not dignify that claim.

HARRIET. / I want your job!

FRANCIS. D-di-did you st-steal fr-fro… /

UNWIN. Not got all day, Francis.

FRANCIS. /…my-my Jude?

HOWE. Never. Never, Francis.

UNWIN. Lie!

MARY COOPER. Francis, don't weep, she's lucky, she's with
our most majestic Father now.

ALL. Amen.

UNWIN. Mary Cooper, this were yer sister.

MARY COOPER. To my knowledge, Howe speaks the truth.
My gripe with Howe, all know is longstanding, 'n' that is his
whistling as he digs a grave.

EDWARD. He does whistle.

MARY COOPER. Quiet, Edward!

EDWARD. Sorry, Mother.

HOWE. Not this again.

MARY COOPER. Dead deserve more respect than a whistle.

HOWE. So I whistle. Try being chipper when all yer see and deal in is death. It be an ask of any man.

MARY COOPER. Knew the risk when thou took on the job, Marshall Howe. Come the day I'm laid to rest I will expect silence. At worse a prayer.

JOHN HANCOCK. Mary, the Reaper's in no rush to claim you. Be many more sexton after Howe before one is finally given task of laying you to rest.

MARY COOPER. If there were one in this village our dear Father would desire closest to him, it is I. Only for sake of this needy boy does he not take me now into his merciful, embracing, arms.

MARY TALBOT *has entered*.

MARY TALBOT. Oh, too late!!

HOWE. Mary Talbot, who else now wants to turn up?

MARY TALBOT. There's plenty more on the way hoping to see Unwin take his beating. I warned yer that would be the case, Unwin!

UNWIN. He's a fucking thief.

WILLIAM. Enough, sir. Denigrating the sanctuary of a church with such vitriol.

UNWIN. What's he saying?

MARY TALBOT. Stop being an arsehole and show God some respect. So what are you two then?

HOWE. New reverend and the wife.

KATHERINE. *Katherine* and William Mompesson.

MARY TALBOT. Ah, come here to take the little we have and gift it to the King?

WILLIAM. We do no such thing.

MARY TALBOT. Yeah and pissing int' wind has never got anyone wet.

UNWIN. Reverend, you don't know what come before, do yer?

WILLIAM. Came before?

UNWIN. Befell Reverend Adams. Nah, he doesn't.

WILLIAM. What befell Reverend Adams?

UNWIN. See not a clue. Should be more cautious of tone yer take with me. Little lamb to a slaughter, you are.

*The* VILLAGERS *tell* UNWIN *to be quiet as…*

MARY TALBOT. He just watched yer get a beating by his sexton, acting the tough man in't really a part yer can play, Unwin.

JOHN SYDALL *enters, the atmosphere changes.*

JOHN SYDALL. What is wrong with your face?

UNWIN. Nothing, Sydall.

HARRIET. He hit him. Lots.

JOHN SYDALL. Is that so?

HOWE. No.

HARRIET. I found his tooth.

JOHN SYDALL. Fighting in front of children? Animals. Bring this village down to the muck pigs wallow in. This will not last. Reckoning is coming.

UNWIN. What form this time, Sydall? Badgers?!

MARY COOPER. Were it not grey squirrels last time!

JOHN SYDALL. Laughter only speeds your descent into hell. Who are you?

KATHERINE. William and Katherine Mompesson.

JOHN SYDALL. What man lets a woman speak for him?

HOWE. This is yer new reverend.

WILLIAM. Reverend William Mompesson.

JOHN SYDALL. Him? You? Ha. Hear this clearly: you are no reverend of mine. Or this village. You hear that?

WILLIAM. Even through the spittle, your point was clear.

KATHERINE. But wrong.

JOHN SYDALL. Wrong?! Hell shall have open arms for all who think so. You come here wishing all to bow to your King. Well know this: God made the men and the devil makes kings. All here must follow the true moral teaching of our Lord Jesus Christ our Saviour. We place our mighty Lord before all others.

HARRIET. Oh. Is that why his wife likes to cuddle that other man, because Sydall wants to bum God more than her?

JOHN HANCOCK. Go home to yer mother, Harriet.

HARRIET. Can I keep yer tooth?

UNWIN. Little use to me now.

HARRIET. And your dead wife's finger?

FRANCIS. Wh-what?

HARRIET. Nothing.

JOHN HANCOCK. Go.

    HARRIET *goes*.

JOHN SYDALL. When Mr Stanley arrives, see how quick you will all be to seek repentance.

    VILLAGERS *all mutter and bicker, it's clearly not the first time this has been said*.

UNWIN. Not this again!

WILLIAM. Who is Mr Stanley?

JOHN SYDALL. He is the true voice of this village.

ELIZABETH HANCOCK. He is the Puritan minister that were evicted.

JOHN SYDALL. Hush your wife, John Hancock.

ELIZABETH HANCOCK. I speak for myself. Truth cannot be silenced.

JOHN SYDALL. This serpent tongue is no greater evident that Mr Stanley's absence has set this village upon path to eternal damnation. Stench of sin rattles the trees.

MARY TALBOT. Oh it is sin, not wind, that be responsible for these leaves.

JOHN SYDALL. And he said: let the women learn in silence with all subjection.

MARY TALBOT. And she said: fuck off.

JOHN SYDALL. Damn thee –

HOWE. Let the dream die, Sydall. It will never happen. Stanley is forbid from ever setting foot in this village.

JOHN SYDALL. Is that so? No. Oh, for so long it were the dream that woke me moist at night but now that dream comes true. Oh, I be in such state of pleasure: Good Anne Stanley is dead!

MARY COOPER. Dead?

EDWARD. God rest her soul.

ALL. Amen.

JOHN SYDALL. And now Mr Stanley comes hence to bury her in the parish that were dearest to her. Oh, look how all the colour drains from your faces. Your days of frivolity are numbered. And yours done here before they even begun. For Mr Stanley will stay beyond.

JOHN HANCOCK. None of this is true.

JOHN SYDALL. God Almighty has your number, John Hancock.

JOHN HANCOCK. Even to bury his wife is to defy the King.

JOHN SYDALL. The King does not live here. This is not London.

KATHERINE. Sir Saville is the only man given power to appoint here.

JOHN SYDALL. Loose-tongued harlot!

WILLIAM. Sir, that is –

JOHN SYDALL. Hear this and hear it only: Saville is in Nottingham. I tire of this governance from afar. Remote hands should not dictate what they cannot see.

JOHN HANCOCK. It is what it is, so now your duty /

JOHN SYDALL. Duty? /

JOHN HANCOCK. / is to accept whoever Sir Saville sends. And they are here now.

JOHN SYDALL. / Duty?! My duty is to my Lord. And he sends Mr Stanley to save Eyam's sins. Not them. There. You, you will be gone before the morn is here, praise God!

JOHN SYDALL *has gone*.

MARY TALBOT. Ignore John Sydall. Seen that man rage at sheep for eating grass.

UNWIN. Used to shit himself drunk every night till he found God.

MARY COOPER. Aye. He talks of sin. Yet under his own roof there is adultery. Promiscuity.

HOWE. Mary, stop slinging rumour.

MARY COOPER. All know the daughter, Emmott, samples more than that baker's bread. And as for his wife and John Wilson.

UNWIN. At it.

JOHN HANCOCK. Do not encourage her.

MARY COOPER. Reverend, it may be our heavenly Father's name we did hear Elizabeth Sydall shouting but it weren't in act of prayer, were it, Edward?

EDWARD. They *were* on their knees.

ELIZABETH HANCOCK. Stop this, Mary. Your gossip could have dire consequence if Sydall were to hear.

MARY COOPER. Or could make him more humble.

ELIZABETH HANCOCK. No. Dire consequence.

WILLIAM. Hello! There is no truth in Mr Sydall's talk of this Reverend Stanley returning?

HOWE. If Good Anne is dead.

EDWARD. God rest her soul.

ALL. Amen.

HOWE. Then he will return. She never wished leave here. A life she'd made.

MARY COOPER. Beyond cruel to have that all taken from her. It is her right to lie eternal in Eyam.

UNWIN. Bury her then go. Stanley is harsher than a pig's bite. Better off with him gone.

MARY TALBOT. Thought the day could never come but I agree with Unwin.

JOHN HANCOCK. Not all think that though. If there is truth in his return then some will demand his stay.

MARY COOPER. I for one.

WILLIAM. But it is not possible. A dissenter is not permitted from returning to where he once preached. It is the law.

HOWE. 'Law'. Really is new here.

VILLAGERS. Aye.

WILLIAM. Would one rather I or soldiers arrive upon your land?

FRANCIS. Stan-Stanley's re-return could cause th-that?

WILLIAM. Think Sir Saville would want the King to learn he harbours a dissenter?

KATHERINE. It will not come to that, will it, William?

WILLIAM. What other action would I have, if I am to be this village's reverend?

MARY TALBOT. Tread careful.

WILLIAM. What?

MARY TALBOT. You heard. No soldiers will ever come on our land again, will they.

UNWIN. No.

HOWE. No.

MARY COOPER. No.

EDWARD. No.

FRANCIS. N-no.

ELIZABETH HANCOCK. No.

MARY TALBOT. John?

JOHN HANCOCK. No. Never again. Regardless of law, it is not possible. How would Stanley afford live? His livery no more.

HOWE. Aye, them now in his old residence.

UNWIN. Sydall would allow him huddle in his bed. Certain of that.

MARY COOPER. There is plenty of space in it, with the gap Elizabeth Sydall leaves.

ELIZABETH HANCOCK. Mary!

JOHN HANCOCK. To stay would require patronage, Sir Saville will not offer that. There is only one in the village who could.

UNWIN. Sheldon.

HOWE. Sheldon is not a man who entertains Sydall's words and ways.

JOHN HANCOCK. Aye. He is as far from a man of God as a man can be.

MARY TALBOT. If God or Stanley is of use, Sheldon will use it. Regardless of what he thinks.

JOHN HANCOCK. Francis, what d'yer know?

FRANCIS. N-nothing. I know noth-nothing.

KATHERINE. We have heard this name, Sheldon, several times, yet not once did Sir Saville make mention of him.

MARY TALBOT. What did Saville tell you of here?

KATHERINE. We know we come to replace Reverend Shoreland Adams.

WILLIAM. It is rather a puzzle, aside from that. As Eyam is not of any standing, a minute village –

MARY COOPER. Heh! Heh! Heh! Heh! Eyam may be small but it is of great significance.

KATHERINE. Naturally. No offence was intended.

ELIZABETH HANCOCK. It is not significant.

MARY COOPER. Elizabeth! This village is all yer know, yet yer speak ill of it. Shame on yer. Now I'll tell yer all about Eyam: best lead yer'll find in whole of Derbyshire, right here, so beautiful yer'd have yer teeth made out of it.

KATHERINE. I see.

MARY COOPER. I haven't finished! Eyam is Sir Saville's only parish for miles, therefore a reflection upon him. The Earl of Cavendish resides at Chatsworth, only five miles from here, and your Saville has got his nose so far up the Earl's arse he can see food every time he takes a bite. This is a surprise?

WILLIAM. Yes. It would make more sense as to why we were sent here.

MARY COOPER. Oh, would it, now we're no longer simply the flies upon a horse's shit.

KATHERINE. We have had a long journey. An upheaval. /

MARY COOPER. Oh yes, from *Yorkshire*.

KATHERINE. / No disrespect was meant at any point. Was it, William?

WILLIAM. No.

MARY COOPER. Well, I might have been a bit overzealous as that is where the good news ends. Tell them about Adams.

JOHN HANCOCK. You do not know the circumstance of his exit?

WILLIAM. Circumstance?

MARY TALBOT. He were hung.

WILLIAM. What?

JOHN HANCOCK. Thank you, Mary. Reverend Adams, he were hung from a tree. Choked till turned blue. Then tethered to his horse, dragged through lanes till his skin were but shreds.

KATHERINE. It cannot be true.

JOHN HANCOCK. Eyam is a village cut off from the world. It's an island. Where isolation lives: discourse, rivalry, friction, they all breed. It can become a law into itself.

WILLIAM. Reverend Adams was hung?

MARY TALBOT. Think we said that pretty clearly.

KATHERINE. Why?

HOWE. He were thought a thief.

KATHERINE. And was he?

HOWE. Yes.

MARY COOPER. And a drunk.

ELIZABETH HANCOCK. Still it were a law taken into its own hand.

WILLIAM. Who did this?

*There are guilty looks from* UNWIN, FRANCIS.

Members of this very room?

UNWIN. I have meat to be delivering.

UNWIN *goes.*

JOHN HANCOCK. People are easily led when scared.

WILLIAM. Who scared them?

EDWARD. The man whose invite you have accepted.

MARY COOPER. Don't go stirring, Edward. Francis, yer never heard Edward speak.

FRANCIS. I… mus-must r-report if – he knew…

MARY COOPER. Francis, he is yer nephew.

FRANCIS *nods*.

Come, Edward, before yer say something more that will land trouble at my door.

MARY COOPER *drags* EDWARD *out*.

HOWE. Bugger this, I am home for me dinner. Reverend, missus: if I see yer in the morn, I see yer in the morn.

HOWE *goes*.

WILLIAM. Nobody attempted to stop this act upon Reverend Adams? No consequence of action met?

ELIZABETH HANCOCK. Where do you think we are, Reverend?

WILLIAM. The answer is becoming clearer to me with every passing moment.

FRANCIS. J-John. Mary. I am sent in-in other r-role (to sp-speak with you on).

JOHN HANCOCK. What now, Francis?

FRANCIS. John, know, I am only the me-messenger –

ELIZABETH HANCOCK. Speak, Francis.

FRANCIS. You k-know what the message is. Do you ac-accept Mr Sh-Sheldon's pr-price?

JOHN HANCOCK. Tell him, the answer is where I left it before – up his dirty bloody arse. Them exact words.

FRANCIS. I, I, I cannot return with that.

WILLIAM. You're not scared of Sheldon?

JOHN HANCOCK. Who would you fear if you were the size of me? We know we do right and he does wrong. And we know God sees that 'n' all.

FRANCIS. M… Mary?

MARY TALBOT. Francis. Know I pity you. A gardener Sheldon employed him, not messenger. All here should know it is not simple. I know without his employment your family will go wanting. They rely upon Sheldon's employment for food, for shelter, for life. As does half, more, of the village. It is not your fault, Francis, that Sheldon exploits you. Knows full well the mines have already broke your body. His power makes victim of you, bids you do work, knowing another will take your job if you do not. Once a man has that hold upon another man he can twist him into any shape.

WILLIAM. You describe a ransom.

JOHN HANCOCK. It is.

KATHERINE. Francis, is it so?

FRANCIS. I can-cannot give you that answer.

KATHERINE. Francis, you are safe here. We are here to aid, to protect you.

FRANCIS. P-please, do not make me lie in a, a, house of God.

WILLIAM. What does Sheldon want with your land?

JOHN HANCOCK. Our holdings may only be small, seven acres combined, but they lie dead centre amongst his land.

MARY TALBOT. We be the shit he must step over. And he's not a man who steps over things.

JOHN HANCOCK. Takes our land it becomes his 'garden', not common land. Gardens can't be mined by anyone but its owner. He wants control of all Eyam's lead. The lifeblood.

KATHERINE. You are quiet, Elizabeth.

ELIZABETH HANCOCK. I'm tired of this. The battle. Every day becomes a greater struggle. My skin is bleached from the ore. John, Mary: is it not time we listened?

JOHN HANCOCK. Listened?

ELIZABETH HANCOCK. He could give us a wage.

MARY TALBOT. Four generations the land has been farmed by Talbots. It were a life I married in to. I knew it to be not easy but were one I proudly chose. To leave the land is to rob my own children of their history.

ELIZABETH HANCOCK. History cannot be used to romance hardship forever. Children, they do not care about the land! What land is it anyway? Lead does not run deep. Grazing is poor. Already we have lost one son, John. Fled for a better life.

JOHN HANCOCK. We do not speak of that!

ELIZABETH HANCOCK. Oh, I am too aware of that. Carry on as we are the other children will follow.

JOHN HANCOCK. This is not for public this talk.

FRANCIS. He does not seek r-remove you. Your home... land, y-you'd be free to-to remain... live as before.

JOHN HANCOCK. Have Sheldon for a landlord! And watch the rents rise year by year. It is our right as free men to have that land. A right I fought for.

ELIZABETH HANCOCK. And look what good that fighting did, another fucking King.

JOHN HANCOCK. I give you my word, here now, under God's roof, Elizabeth, I would sooner soak my hands in Sheldon's blood than sell my land to him.

ELIZABETH HANCOCK. Once, John, you would have said our land.

JOHN HANCOCK. Once you would have never thought to leave it.

ELIZABETH HANCOCK. Time's a bastard then, in't it.

*ELIZABETH HANCOCK goes.*

KATHERINE. I hope that we can count you as a friend in this journey.

JOHN HANCOCK. Reverend Adams also asked me that. I shook his hand. Let your actions speak for our friendship.

*And with that,* JOHN HANCOCK *goes.*

MARY TALBOT. Come Francis, they have enough food for thought to sustain 'em for months.

FRANCIS. You-you will still a-attend Mr Shel-Sheldon? Rev-Reverend?

KATHERINE. We shall.

MARY TALBOT. Reverend. Mrs Mompesson. Welcome to Eyam.

MARY TALBOT *and* FRANCIS *leave*.

WILLIAM. Katherine, we are to leave now.

KATHERINE. Leave?

WILLIAM. They hung my predecessor from a tree. Hung him! What people do this?

KATHERINE. Those in need of guidance.

WILLIAM. In need of the law.

KATHERINE. God has sent us here for a reason, I know it. We are going to go and meet this Mr Sheldon.

WILLIAM. So my neck can be measured for a noose.

KATHERINE. William, where is the considered man I know? We have yet to meet this man they paint a monster, yet you believe all that is said. Come, William, remember every story has two sides.

WILLIAM. I know, I know.

KATHERINE. Then be so good as to live by that belief.

JOHN WILSON *enters. He is gently beckoning to a person who has yet to join us*.

JOHN WILSON. Hello. We hoped to speak to the new reverend and his wife.

WILLIAM. Oh, what now?!

KATHERINE. That is us.

JOHN WILSON. We do not mean to disturb.

KATHERINE. You do no such thing. William?

WILLIAM. You are?

JOHN WILSON. John Wilson. And Elizabeth –

WILLIAM. Elizabeth! This village appears to be populated solely with Johns or Elizabeths or Marys. Is it a trick that everyone is playing upon us and really all go by different names?

JOHN WILSON. No. It's just what people are called.

KATHERINE. Strong, solid names.

JOHN WILSON. Elizabeth, this is the new reverend and his wife.

ELIZABETH SYDALL *has joined them.*

KATHERINE. Mr and Mrs Wilson, how may we help?

ELIZABETH SYDALL. Pray stop, I am not Mrs Wilson. I am Elizabeth Sydall.

KATHERINE. Forgive me, my assumption were that you were married.

ELIZABETH SYDALL. Do not let my husband know that were your assumption.

KATHERINE. You have our word. How may we help?

ELIZABETH SYDALL. You have children?

KATHERINE. We do. Two. A boy and a girl. They will arrive imminent. Every day their absence pains us.

ELIZABETH SYDALL.…A child is a blessing, Reverend. A gift from our Lord. Six beautiful most precious gifts he has blessed upon me…

WILLIAM. Are we to assume his plan has not stopped at six?

ELIZABETH SYDALL. I am with child. Seven, sir. Seven children… Seven! I… Seven!! Seven, John, seven – I never said it out loud before. Seven!

KATHERINE. God has granted you great strength.

JOHN WILSON. Elizabeth is a true marvel. Not one lost in gestation, birth or life. Shhh, now, Elizabeth.

WILLIAM. Praise God.

KATHERINE. What of your husband?

ELIZABETH SYDALL. He remains unaware, as yet.

WILLIAM. Do you fear his response?

JOHN WILSON. You had pleasure of meeting him earlier, I understand. John Sydall.

KATHERINE. John Sydall is your husband?

JOHN WILSON. It is not a pleasure, I know not why I said pleasure because it is none. So little pleasure you might never want to spend time with him. Even a wife might think the same.

WILLIAM. I see.

KATHERINE. William, I wonder if you truly do. Elizabeth? We are not here as judges.

ELIZABETH SYDALL. There has not been any laying in the marital bed.

KATHERINE. None?

ELIZABETH SYDALL. Forgive me, I did try to entice him. A trick. But he became angered. Scalded my wantonness. Before it only ever were in the dark he'd visit.

WILLIAM. There is no need for extra detail. We do follow.

JOHN WILSON. The seventh will if anything be the first.

ELIZABETH SYDALL. This is a lifetime in waiting. But that is no excuse. We are sinners. We know that.

WILLIAM. If you seek forgiveness, God is merciful.

ELIZABETH SYDALL. It would be a lie.

JOHN WILSON. God will punish us as he sees fit. But we do not wish him punish a life that has had no complicity in its creation.

KATHERINE. How can we help?

JOHN WILSON. John Sydall is a cruel, cruel man.

ELIZABETH SYDALL. A bastard. He can never know. And therefore we do not know what to do.

WILLIAM. We will pray for you.

JOHN WILSON. Pray?

WILLIAM. Prayer is all we can offer.

ELIZABETH SYDALL. We thank you for them.

JOHN WILSON. Come, we have taken enough of the
Reverend's time.

*They go.*

KATHERINE. They leave more bereft, vulnerable, than whence
they arrived.

WILLIAM. I am instructed to tell them their behaviour is
unholy. That they have committed sin.

KATHERINE. They know, William. They know all this.

WILLIAM. What would you have me do? Am I to encourage
her to seduce her husband? To advocate adultery? What?

KATHERINE. We are not here to judge but to comfort.

WILLIAM. You think I failed them? I offer silence and prayer.
A puritan would have had them dragged before the
congregation. Vilified. Destroyed.

KATHERINE. William, that is no comparison to boast upon.

WILLIAM. Sir Saville has sent us head first into a hurricane of
festering excrement.

KATHERINE. Even if this is a village in the mire –

WILLIAM. Mire? Fighting and fornication appears more casual
than any sport I ever saw play. Forget this meeting with
Sheldon, I will ride to Sir Saville immediate.

KATHERINE. William, you gave that man, Francis, your word
we will attend. I have never known you break your word.
There is no finer, more attractive, quality than that.

WILLIAM. ... Well that is just...

KATHERINE. A wife knowing how to win.

*And with that,* KATHERINE *exits.* WILLIAM *considers.
The crow cries. He curses it. Exits.*

*The crow turns as* GEORGE VICCARS *walks through the
village.*

*Another crow and then another appear. They watch*
VICCARS.

*The angel of death.*

**3.**

COOPERS' *cottage.*

*A knock at the door.*

MARY COOPER. Think a door opens itself. Edward, go attend.

EDWARD *goes to the door.* VICCARS *is in the doorway.*

EDWARD. Evening.

VICCARS. Good evening.

MARY COOPER. Who is it, Edward?

EDWARD. I do not know.

VICCARS. I come about the room.

EDWARD. Room?

MARY COOPER. Ah let him in. What is it about Eyam and new
arrivals today: like a shit after a feast, it all comes at once.

EDWARD. Mother, what is this?

MARY COOPER. We require a lodger to help meet our shortfall.

EDWARD. Shortfall?

MARY COOPER. Think the food you scoff comes free? The
wood to warm your toes? No, it costs and you contribute
nothing, yet expect everything.

EDWARD. Where do you intend him to lodge?... There is only
my room...

MARY COOPER. We all must make sacrifices.

VICCARS. I mean no intrusion.

MARY COOPER. Name.

VICCARS. George Viccars.

MARY COOPER. Mr Viccars, you'll soon learn to ignore my son. You have employment?

VICCARS. I do, yes.

MARY COOPER. Finally what this house needs – a working man. Trade?

VICCARS. I am a tailor. My life is spent upon the road.

EDWARD. Where have you been?

MARY COOPER. Hush, Edward. This is no shop. Customers will not be received. Vultures, snooping, passing judgement on my home.

VICCARS. Very well. I require little in the way of space. A table and light, a candle if dark, is all I ask.

MARY COOPER. You were told the rate?

VICCARS. I was, yes.

MARY COOPER. Two weeks in advance.

VICCARS. You wish to count it?

MARY COOPER. Put it in my hand.

> VICCARS *does*. MARY COOPER *counts the money.* VICCARS *and* EDWARD *exchange a glance.*

Edward, show Mr Viccars to his room.

EDWARD. Yes, Mother.

VICCARS. Thank you, Edward.

> EDWARD *leads* VICCARS *through the house.*

**4.**

*The* SHELDONS'. SHELDON *stares out of the window.*
*A luxurious rug covers the floor.* ELIZABETH SHELDON
*enters wearing a new dress, she waits for him to take notice.*
*She repeats the process, her sighs becoming more and more*
*dramatic.*

ELIZABETH SHELDON. Must I come in then out again! Back
and forth! Philip, I put this on for you, as you did request.

SHELDON *turns*.

SHELDON. So you have.

ELIZABETH SHELDON. Is that all I warrant? A 'so you
have'. Where is the ooh, the ah?!

SHELDON. Have you looked in the mirror?

ELIZABETH SHELDON. I have.

SHELDON. Then you know the answer.

*She looks in the mirror again.*

ELIZABETH SHELDON. I do know the answer. I thought
tonight a night for trying. Together. In our marital bed. But
I will happily retire with what I behold in the mirror.

*She walks to the mirror and kisses her reflection.*

Expect triplets by the time I am finished with you.

SHELDON. Save your smut.

ELIZABETH SHELDON. For who? Come to bed.

SHELDON. No.

ELIZABETH SHELDON. Please.

SHELDON. Begging does little for me.

ELIZABETH SHELDON. Not begging, it is necessity, I need
you to remove me from this. What is all this for? This empire
you seek to build, if there is no one left to leave it to? I need
a child.

SHELDON. Yes, you do.

ELIZABETH SHELDON. Come then. Pretend I am John Hancock – if it is anger that you have to burn.

SHELDON *grabs hold of* ELIZABETH SHELDON. *She stares him down.*

I will never sell my land to you, Sheldon. You pig.

SHELDON. Watch your mouth, Hancock.

ELIZABETH SHELDON. Make me.

JOHN SYDALL *enters.*

Oh, God, it is him – there goes my night!

JOHN SYDALL. Mrs Sheldon, late for intrusion I know.

ELIZABETH SHELDON. Save it. How quick a flood can turn to drought.

SHELDON. What is it, Sydall?

JOHN SYDALL. The devil is quick to send his minions.

SHELDON. Reverend Mompesson?

JOHN SYDALL. Aye. The false prophet walks amongst us. Jezebel at his side.

ELIZABETH SHELDON. What are they like?

JOHN SYDALL. Vile. He is a King's man. She has a brazen and unchecked tongue. If it weren't for Mr Stanley's imminent arrival my torch would be lit ready to drive them from our village gates. /

ELIZABETH SHELDON. This village has no gates.

JOHN SYDALL. / God be the only law that exists here, not the whim of a harlot King.

SHELDON. Amen.

JOHN SYDALL. I continue to share such words amongst the village.

SHELDON. Good man.

JOHN SYDALL. Nothing pleases me more. This village craves Mr Stanley's vision.

SHELDON. Amen. Stanley shall have my full support, patronage.

JOHN SYDALL. Praise God.

SHELDON. Always it shall be to him the village turns for guidance, not Sir Saville's appointed man.

JOHN SYDALL. I feel the light of our Lord returning. The battle between good and evil does begin here in Eyam. Mr Sheldon, the rapture, it commences here today!

SHELDON. Amen. Now go make all village aware that Stanley is returning.

JOHN SYDALL. Each time I utter Mr Stanley's name it shall bring me closer to most majestic climax!

JOHN SYDALL *exits*.

ELIZABETH SHELDON. Amen, amen, amen. Why must you entertain that man?

SHELDON. Zealots have uses.

ELIZABETH SHELDON. Making skin crawl. I detest him coming here.

SHELDON. It is no joy for me either.

ELIZABETH SHELDON. It's not your chest he stares at.

SHELDON. Look out there. Remember that pit I dragged you from? That life?

ELIZABETH SHELDON. Vividly.

SHELDON. Since Stanley's departure, those animals have become emboldened. They no longer fear God. It is as if God is their friend, not master. Saville's appointment will only fuel that fire. With that they question. Question my right to land. When it is my land that provides them a living. Without me they couldn't eat, sleep under a roof, even take a shit. I rebuilt Eyam – no one else – me. I will not have Saville, a man who has never once set foot upon this land, claim it simply because his great-great-grandfather once kissed a king's arse.

JOHN SYDALL *re-enters with* MR THOMAS STANLEY.

JOHN SYDALL. Mr Stanley is here! Here! Finally! Mark me weak but I feared this day would never come. To see you stood here again my whole body is awoken with joy. Praise God! No longer are we abandoned.

STANLEY. It were no abandonment. No choice were given. Banished, from our own home.

JOHN SYDALL. A crime that will long echo throughout this land.

STANLEY. Man will come and his laws will go. His weakness will bring his own destruction but God is always present.

JOHN SYDALL. Amen. The only solace I take for Good Anne's death is that she never did see the state Eyam befalls. God's embrace is the greatest blessing to be bestowed upon mankind.

STANLEY. Amen.

JOHN SYDALL. Good Anne's death shall offer salvation to all. For it is the light that leads you back.

STANLEY. Even in death she still does God's work.

JOHN SYDALL. Amen. Praise our heavenly Father for taking her so.

STANLEY. Amen.

SHELDON. Leave us now, Sydall.

JOHN SYDALL. Not yet. Mr Stanley requires me list him all the places where sin has lain.

SHELDON *clicks his fingers*.

SHELDON. Now.

JOHN SYDALL. I fear no man but God. Remember that when you click your fingers.

SHELDON. You think you be closer to God than all here, Sydall? Moral Sydall, a saint who knows no sin! Ha! Look under your own roof – at your daughter. Come back to me when she's not riding that baker's cock, then say God protects such a man. A man who breeds whores. Now fuck off.

JOHN SYDALL *looks to* STANLEY, STANLEY *ignores him.* JOHN SYDALL *goes.*

Mr Stanley. Welcome.

STANLEY. Mr Sheldon.

SHELDON *becomes aware of what he is standing on. A luxurious rug.*

SHELDON. Arctic fox. Several if truth be told. Go ahead. Touch it. I have been known lie upon it. Soak up its warmth. Truly divine.

STANLEY. A man could live his whole life and not sleep on something as luxurious. Yet you use it for your feet. Time has clearly been generous.

SHELDON. Nor does it diminish what memories I hold of you. Thomas, I delight to see you here returned. We must celebrate, a glass of wine?

ELIZABETH SYDALL *enters with wine.*

STANLEY. No.

SHELDON. You will taste none finer.

STANLEY. I have no doubt, but no.

SHELDON. We did use to share a glass or two. Dear Anne was partial to a drop if I recall.

STANLEY. Those days are long past.

SHELDON. Indeed. Where is your wife, Thomas? Upon the carriage?

STANLEY. She will be buried hence.

SHELDON. You plan to bury at this hour? In the dark? Wait till the morrow. The sun, the birds, friends. A fitting send-off. Till then have a drink. Enjoy your return. Worry not, suitable arrangements have been made to accommodate.

SHELDON *gestures for* ELIZABETH SYDALL *to put the wine in front of* STANLEY. *She does and with that she can finally leave.*

STANLEY. I said no.

SHELDON. You have simple needs like me. All I need is a view and good news. There is the view, which leaves only the good news: Thomas, your wife is dead.

STANLEY. She rests now.

SHELDON. Amen. Permit me to introduce my wife, Elizabeth Sheldon.

STANLEY. Mrs Sheldon, we have met before, but I believe by different name.

ELIZABETH SHELDON. Moseley, sir. My first husband were Mr James Moseley, of Tideswell. He did pass two years prior. Mr Stanley, I am terribly sorry for your loss.

STANLEY. Do not be, she is with our heavenly Father now.

ELIZABETH SHELDON. You will be told it gets easier.

STANLEY. And here you are, my proof. Remarried.

ELIZABETH SHELDON. Mr Stanley, my husband is buried near. It gives comfort to not be afar.

STANLEY. Is that so.

ELIZABETH SHELDON. Yes. To be able to visit, or lay a flower. Does the thought of being removed from where Anne rests not bring pain?

STANLEY. I will call upon God to provide the strength.

ELIZABETH SHELDON. Where then, if not this village, will you go?

STANLEY. God will guide me.

ELIZABETH SHELDON. He guides you now, Mr Stanley. Here.

SHELDON. Thomas, how intend you to survive? This barbaric act of uniformity strips you of livery.

STANLEY. I am rich in the love of God.

SHELDON. Don't be a fool, winter will still strike you dead with no roof above your head.

STANLEY. If that be God's plan, it be his plan.

SHELDON. That is no plan that is simply waste. Thomas, you still wish to speak the word of the Lord our Saviour?

STANLEY. It is why God did put me upon this earth.

SHELDON. Indeed. Tell me where else can you go and share the word of God? Nowhere. Only here can you be offered that.

ELIZABETH SHELDON. And think on your dearest Anne. You do not wish her buried in a place of sin.

SHELDON. Heaven forbid. Eyam necessitates your intervention. Returned to what it were. Only then may Good Anne lay in eternal peace.

ELIZABETH SHELDON. Amen.

SHELDON. No answer is required now. Sleep upon it. In comfort. Now, Thomas, there be a cuckoo in your nest.

STANLEY. Saville's new man?

SHELDON. But fear not, he'll soon be gone.

ELIZABETH SYDALL *enters*.

ELIZABETH SYDALL. Sir, Reverend Mompesson and his wife are here.

SHELDON. How fortuitous. Send them in.

KATHERINE *and* WILLIAM *enter*. ELIZABETH SYDALL *then leaves*.

Philip Sheldon, and you must be Saville's appointed man.

WILLIAM. I say God's appointed man foremostly.

SHELDON. Oh my, that is encouraging, an actual man of conviction Saville sends us. Reverend William Mompesson and your good wife Katherine, I believe.

KATHERINE. Mr Sheldon. You received Sir Saville's correspondence?

SHELDON. I was made aware of the news.

WILLIAM. It appears others weren't.

SHELDON. You arrive at a very delicate moment in this village's history.

KATHERINE. We are aware.

SHELDON. Many still sore from the actions of Reverend Adams, a man Saville demand they trust. Why worry those people?

WILLIAM. You think our arrival a worry?

SHELDON. Let's see how you fare. Where are the children? You have children, don't you?

KATHERINE. We do.

SHELDON. A boy and girl, yes.

KATHERINE. Yes.

SHELDON. Yet only the two of you travel?

KATHERINE. Yes.

WILLIAM. They are with family.

KATHERINE. Once we're settled they will be sent for.

SHELDON. How astute. Why disrupt a child? Carting them here, oh the upheaval. And, oh, imagine after all that you never felt settled. Yes, very astute. This is my wife. Elizabeth.

ELIZABETH SHELDON. Welcome –

SHELDON. Wife, go show Mrs Mompesson your dresses or other pretty things.

KATHERINE. That will not be necessary.

SHELDON. She doesn't care for clothes, your wife?

KATHERINE. Clothes do not require my care, the parishioners do. You must be Reverend Thomas Stanley?

STANLEY. I am no reverend.

SHELDON. True, Mr Stanley, does not require such grand titling to know his connection to God. Thomas, these are the people that wish to occupy the bed you and your dearest Anne did sleep in.

KATHERINE. We are deeply sorry for your loss.

STANLEY. Why? She is with our majestic Father now.

WILLIAM. I am glad that brings you comfort.

STANLEY. Comfort is a luxury I do not require.

WILLIAM. What is your intention, Reverend? Wish to make Eyam a home again? Or will you depart once you have seen to your wife's burial?

SHELDON. Excellent question, Reverend.

FRANCIS *enters*.

Francis, what has been said about you and this house!

FRANCIS. Un-unless it is on f-fire not t-to come in.

SHELDON. And still you stand here.

FRANCIS. S-sor-sorry. Mr Unwin is here, sir. Wan-wanting payment f-for deer he brings.

SHELDON. What are you waiting for, bring him and the deer through!

FRANCIS *exits*.

WILLIAM. Reverend?

STANLEY. It is my understanding that sin now makes its home within Eyam. How can I allow Good Anne to rest in soil so tainted?

WILLIAM. You plan to stay?

KATHERINE. How will that be possible?

SHELDON. The Lord provides.

UNWIN *enters, followed by* FRANCIS, *labouring under the weight of a deer, still in its hide*.

UNWIN. Hurry up, Francis!

FRANCIS. I'm c-coming.

UNWIN. Francis, if you drop that /

FRANCIS. Awf-ful h-heavy. My b-back is giv-giving way.

UNWIN. / majestic animal, it'll be you getting skinned instead. Mr and Mrs Sheldon. Reverends. A right noble beast, I have for yer. It were not easy to come by. Be reflected in price. Oh my, is this arctic fox?

SHELDON. Get off it. There's enough arseholes on there as it is.

UNWIN *does*.

Thomas, venison I recall were your favourite. This here is my gift to the village. A communal feast, no better way to celebrate your return.

UNWIN. No gift until I've been paid.

SHELDON. Unwin, the village is in need of a meal fitting for Mr Stanley's return.

UNWIN. Pay me then wear it as a cape for all I care. Francis, take it back out.

SHELDON. Francis, put it down.

UNWIN. Francis, who said you could put that down!? Where's my money?

SHELDON. You'll get paid. Don't you butcher it before you sell?

UNWIN. Aye.

SHELDON *hands over money*.

SHELDON. Get on with it then.

UNWIN. Here?

SHELDON. Where else?

ELIZABETH SHELDON. Outside. Or in the kitchens!

SHELDON. Do it here.

UNWIN *shrugs and takes out a knife*.

Not on the rug! Move the rug, Francis!

FRANCIS. Y-yes, sir.

FRANCIS *moves the rug*.

SHELDON. You're not squeamish, are you? There may be a little blood is all.

KATHERINE. Is this your act?

SHELDON. Act?

KATHERINE. A show especially for us? Made to intimidate?

UNWIN. Go get the bucket, Francis. This will be messy.

FRANCIS *gets the bucket. And it will prove to be messy:*
FRANCIS *will become covered in blood.*

SHELDON. Intimidation?

KATHERINE. We have learnt of what befell Reverend Adams.

SHELDON. Ah, thief Adams, the wolf in sheep's clothing. He did leave in a rather abrupt manner.

WILLIAM. Abrupt? He were hung and dragged through the village.

SHELDON. That is a dramatic interpretation.

WILLIAM. Is it a lie?

SHELDON. Are you here to cause problems?

WILLIAM. I am appointed by Sir Saville, by the right of His Majesty Charles the Second to serve this parish –

SHELDON. Is the King here? Oh, is he? And Saville? Should I check outside, they could be parked on 'I Don't Give a Fuck' Lane.

WILLIAM. We have been sent to serve God.

SHELDON. There is nothing more noble than what you speak.

WILLIAM. It will be impossible to do so if Reverend Stanley remains.

SHELDON. You would evict a widow from the village that he has given all his life to?

WILLIAM. It is the law. It is apparent that there is a rotten core in this village.

SHELDON. I would agree. Oh, is it me? Is that what all are saying?

WILLIAM. No.

SHELDON. No? But you seemed certain. Who has said so? I can guess. Guessing is one of my most favoured ways to spend an hour. Mary Cooper? Mary Talbot? Elizabeth Hancock? Elizabeth Sydall?

WILLIAM. You will be good to these people.

SHELDON. Elizabeth Sydall.

WILLIAM. You will be good to Elizabeth Sydall.

SHELDON. Will I?

WILLIAM. That is what she needs.

KATHERINE. It is what all need.

SHELDON *clicks his fingers*.

SHELDON. Elizabeth. Come here.

ELIZABETH SYDALL *enters*.

ELIZABETH SYDALL. Yes, sir?

SHELDON. Relax, Elizabeth, friendly tête-á-tête is all this be. Did you visit Reverend Mompesson?

ELIZABETH SYDALL. Our paths met in passing.

SHELDON. Oh dear, lying is not your forte.

WILLIAM. Indeed. Passing is all.

SHELDON. No, no, no, see he has asked me to be particularly kind to you. /

WILLIAM. To all.

SHELDON. / Kind, Elizabeth, am I not kind?

ELIZABETH SYDALL. Epitome of the word.

SHELDON. Clear contradiction here. As obviously, something prompted that from him, something you said.

ELIZABETH SYDALL. No, sir.

SHELDON. Filling out, aren't you. A real goer. Who would have thought Sydall had it in him. /

WILLIAM. Refrain from such vulgarity.

SHELDON. / Have you never thought to put a cork up it, Elizabeth?

ELIZABETH SYDALL. I'm sorry, sir?

SHELDON. To squeeze it out. Sydall's seed when he dumps it inside you.

STANLEY. Enough.

SHELDON. Elizabeth, does the world really need another wretched sprog from your loins? Another burden for me to carry? /

KATHERINE. Cease now.

ELIZABETH SHELDON. Philip –

SHELDON. / Because that is what you would ask, you would be wishing me carry the weight of that thing.

ELIZABETH SYDALL. No.

SHELDON. You do not need my employment?

ELIZABETH SYDALL. Greatly do. But there is no child, sir.

SHELDON. No? Just a bit fat then?

ELIZABETH SYDALL. Yes.

SHELDON. Obviously paying you too much. Plumping you up on my coin. Wages will be adjusted so.

ELIZABETH SYDALL. As you wish.

WILLIAM. Enough is enough.

SHELDON. What do you think, Thomas?

STANLEY. The point you wished make has been made.

SHELDON. That will be all.

ELIZABETH SYDALL. All?

SHELDON. Yes, Elizabeth Sydall, all.

ELIZABETH SYDALL *goes.*

KATHERINE. That amused you?

SHELDON. Oh, lighten up.

KATHERINE. I will not lighten up.

WILLIAM. You wonder where sin lies in this village, Reverend? Is it not here, the man who would wish you be his guest.

SHELDON. Such vigour. What collar size do you think he is, wife?

ELIZABETH SHELDON. It is not for me to say.

SHELDON. Unwin, your knife.

> UNWIN *hands it over.* SHELDON *weighs it up. He then cuts into the deer. He pulls out the deer's heart. He holds it up.*

That deer is Eyam. This is me. Nothing exists without me. No life goes untouched. I am the only reason it lives.

WILLIAM. Katherine, we are to go.

SHELDON. That's right, walk away. Eyam is not to be your home.

WILLIAM. Maybe you shall succeed in driving us away. But we won't be the last that Sir Saville sends here.

SHELDON. That poncey high-born fucker knows nothing of this world.

WILLIAM. Whatever hatred you carry for Sir Saville, know that this home of yours, it would not account for one of his wings. In the world of money you are nothing. And if that, money, is your God, then know you have already lost. Sir Saville will always be your victor. Come, Katherine, each passing moment in this room my soul does ebb.

KATHERINE. You didn't take that animal's life, you hacked its carcass apart. You're simply a butcher.

*They exit. A moment of silence.*

SHELDON. Francis, get that fucking carcass out of my sight!

FRANCIS. W-where?

SHELDON. I don't care. Out there. Out of my sight. And if there be any blood upon my floor you will know of it. Now! What?

UNWIN. My knife.

*As* FRANCIS *takes the deer away,* SHELDON *considers. Eventually hands it back to* UNWIN.

She flattered you. You ain't no butcher.

UNWIN *exits*.

SHELDON. What?

STANLEY. Is there truth in what was said? Of Reverend Adams?

SHELDON. We're not so different, Thomas.

STANLEY. I am a man of God.

SHELDON. God. God! Uhhh!

STANLEY. Do not take the Lord's name in vain.

SHELDON. Oh, Thomas, that does not work for me. I do not buy what you sell. God is nothing to me.

ELIZABETH SHELDON. He does not speak for us both.

SHELDON. Woman, out.

ELIZABETH SHELDON....

*She exits*.

SHELDON. We trade in fear, Thomas, fear is our friend. God is a way to keep people poor. That is all.

STANLEY. Base lie.

SHELDON. Misery is the life you sell them.

STANLEY. Hush, man!

SHELDON. Hush, in my own home!

STANLEY. For he flattereth himself in his own eyes, until his iniquity be found to be hateful.

SHELDON. To some I'm certain that would strike fear, make some sense.

STANLEY. Servitude is not misery. The promise of God's love is hope. Enriches all. Man cannot live in the pleasures of the world and live in joy in heaven –

SHELDON. Do you wish to stay?

STANLEY. How can I leave Eyam in such state?

SHELDON. Then remember the cottage, the food, the wine that is on my tab not God's. That's right, it's mine. It suit both of us if people do not question what we state. Now, go forth and earn your fucking keep!

*And with that* STANLEY *exits.*

## 5.

*Village.*

WILLIAM *and* KATHERINE.

WILLIAM. At least we have yet to even unpack our possessions. If we are quick we will make Sheffield before the sun sets.

KATHERINE. That's it then, is it? Your fight gone?

WILLIAM. Fight, I didn't come here to fight. I came here duped. Under the impression I would lead.

KATHERINE. This is where we are meant to be, William. That man, Sheldon, he does not rule us.

WILLIAM. He would snuff us out in our very own beds.

KATHERINE. Do not tell me you fear that ungodly creature.

WILLIAM. You would have our children live in his shadow?

KATHERINE. I would have our children see that men who act with such villainy do not prosper.

WILLIAM. Are you serious?

KATHERINE. I have never had you marked as a coward, William.

WILLIAM. That is unfair.

KATHERINE. You always talked of hope. Of what a united community can do. Why now shirk from the challenge?

WILLIAM. There is another in our own nest.

KATHERINE. God will guide you and it will pass.

WILLIAM. It will not pass. If I allow a Puritan to remain, it is me that the law will strike down on.

KATHERINE. Together and with God's strength this can be solved. I know it. William?

EMMOTT SYDALL *enters. A bundle of energy.*

EMMOTT. You're the new reverend.

KATHERINE. He is.

EMMOTT. I'm Emmott.

WILLIAM. Emmott.

EMMOTT. Know like others you will not find me a stranger. And I will be open.

KATHERINE. And you shall always have our time.

EMMOTT. Let us start now then. I am in love.

WILLIAM. Love?

KATHERINE. That is good.

EMMOTT. And I want you to marry me to the man. Rowland Torre. I know, Rowland, it is not a name given to the knight who rescues a princess from her tower, and I say man but yet he cannot even grow a wisp under his chin, but oh he does make my skin burn and dance as if it's wrought with fever! Oh, Reverend, that look you give! Do not fear, we have only met for stolen words and kisses. I am still a maid. He bakes me bread, Reverend. Bread! No knight would e'er do that.

WILLIAM. I don't doubt. Emmott, you are how old?

EMMOTT. Age? Age is irrelevant. I know what I feel. Do you not remember first love? That is too long a pause! Reverend, do you even love your wife?!

WILLIAM. She is my wife.

EMMOTT. That is your answer?

KATHERINE. William?

WILLIAM. For a woman who sees marriage as love I thought that should suffice.

EMMOTT. Then you do understand! Reverend, I have been told stories by men who pass by in trade that times move forward outside our little world. That now we no longer should live as if under the cloud of eternal damnation. That hope is what men such as you preach. That life can be lived, love can be shared!

WILLIAM. We are very far from London here.

EMMOTT. I do not ask permission to raise my skirt to every man, Reverend.

WILLIAM. Emmott –

EMMOTT. I simply ask to be made a wife! Is that a sin?!

WILLIAM. No.

EMMOTT. Then help me. Please, Reverend, sway my father's objections.

KATHERINE. Ah, is John Sydall your father?

EMMOTT. From that tone I assume he's already crossed your path.

WILLIAM. He did make himself acquainted.

KATHERINE. On what grounds does your father object?

EMMOTT. Every day will bring a different reason. His hair does have too much shine, his floury hands, being from Stoney Middleton –

WILLIAM. Emmott, be honest with me.

EMMOTT. I love my family. I do not want to be a memory. A memory that his words shape. Should I wish, I want to be able to return to them. Will you speak to him?

WILLIAM. Very well.

EMMOTT. Hear that, Rowland. He will speak to him.

ROWLAND TORRE *enters*. EMMOTT *jumps into his arms*.

I told you there was hope. I knew it. Felt it. I can feel it now.

KATHERINE. I'm certain you can.

EMMOTT. Oh, Rowland, we are to be married!

WILLIAM. Let us take it step by step.

ROWLAND. Perhaps it is best if I put you down.

*He does*.

Reverend. Mrs Reverend. I do love Emmott.

EMMOTT. Nightingales could not sing as sweet a note.

KATHERINE. William, they make a rather sweet couple.

WILLIAM. Young.

KATHERINE. We were little older when we first met.

EMMOTT. Ha! You will find some here cling to past. Scared of change. Others though we know the wheels turn and the past is past. We want a new future. You will help us do that.

KATHERINE. Emmott, you offer the welcome that we hoped and one that we wish to deliver upon, don't we, William?

WILLIAM. Nothing is more necessary than hope.

JOHN SYDALL (*off*). Emmott!

ROWLAND. That is your father.

JOHN SYDALL (*off*). Emmott! Show yourself!

ELIZABETH SYDALL *races in*.

ELIZABETH SYDALL. Emmott, quick, your father, he has heard the news.

ROWLAND. About us?

EMMOTT. Well I will not hide from him.

ELIZABETH SYDALL. This is not the time, Emmott.

EMMOTT. When will be the time then?

ELIZABETH SYDALL. Stop that.

EMMOTT. I will not live like you – living in fear, afraid of my heart.

ROWLAND. Emmott –

EMMOTT. No, Rowland, we do this now or never.

JOHN SYDALL *enters*.

JOHN SYDALL. Inside. Now, girl.

EMMOTT. What can be said can be said here.

JOHN SYDALL…. You!

EMMOTT. He is with me.

SYDALL. Do you not speak for yourself?

ROWLAND. Mr Sydall, I do not wish to be on bad terms with you.

JOHN SYDALL. Yet you… sully… my daughter… your sordid rendezvous, I know of them!

EMMOTT. Only an idiot would not. We have not made it a secret.

JOHN SYDALL. God strike thee down!

ELIZABETH SYDALL. Rowland is a good man.

JOHN SYDALL. Good! Him! The man who has made our daughter a whore!

EMMOTT. If you think that love makes me a whore, then that is what I am. A whore. Your daughter is a whore.

JOHN SYDALL *goes to grab* EMMOTT.

ROWLAND. Do not touch her!

EMMOTT. Let him. /

ELIZABETH SYDALL. John, enough!

EMMOTT. / Let all here see what he is!

*They manage to hold* JOHN SYDALL *back*.

The reverend will see us married.

JOHN SYDALL. Marry her? It is the devil you act for, not our heavenly Father.

WILLIAM. I have not agreed to this.

EMMOTT. What?

KATHERINE. William?

EMMOTT. Tell him, Reverend – that you will marry us. Tell him! Liar.

WILLIAM. Emmott.

JOHN SYDALL. A noose is too good for you, sinner!

EMMOTT. I am going to marry this man.

JOHN SYDALL. Over my dead body.

EMMOTT. So be it.

*Again* JOHN SYDALL *attempts to grab* EMMOTT. ROWLAND *pushes him to the floor.* JOHN SYDALL *stays there.*

ROWLAND. I hoped to have your blessing.

JOHN SYDALL. Never.

EMMOTT. Then that is your choice.

ROWLAND. I love your daughter.

JOHN SYDALL. Love, what does a baker know of love?

EMMOTT. More than a father ever will. Rowland and I will share our lives till our bones lie side by side in clouds of nought but dust.

JOHN SYDALL. Then you will not be looking up at this sky. You are disowned. Never set foot in this village ever again. And may God punish you justly!

JOHN SYDALL *starts to exit.*

ELIZABETH SYDALL. He does not mean it, Emmott.

JOHN SYDALL. Oh, I do. I do! Woman. Home.

EMMOTT. Mother?

*A moment.* ELIZABETH SYDALL *has to follow* JOHN SYDALL.

It is a lie then, Reverend – you offer nothing new. The same old world that we have always lived in. Where is the hope?

EMMOTT *and* ROWLAND *go.* WILLIAM *and* KATHERINE *remain.*

KATHERINE. Emmott could not have said it better. Where is the hope, William? Where are you?

WILLIAM. I'm in Eyam – where hope dies!

KATHERINE. Enough! There are people here for whom we can be of true help.

WILLIAM. They were young, hot-headed –

KATHERINE. Do not dismiss the young. Hear yourself, William! The words you say.

WILLIAM. That look you give, what is it?

KATHERINE. It tells a story that you have to ask.

WILLIAM. Disappointment. It is that. Say it is not that. Why is this so important to you? What do you see in this place?

KATHERINE. It is the right thing.

WILLIAM. Be truthful, Katherine.

KATHERINE. If we were to leave, what? Go where? Return to where everyone knew me? It is very well for you to think on that option. There you were respected. There I was simply your ill wife. So yes, I wish to start again. To not be defined by a memory of a woman not well. Here, I can be of use. And if that is not enough for you then I never know what will.

WILLIAM *nods.*

**6.**

*Suddenly we are at the Delph, Eyam.*

EMMOTT *stands in the alcove. She tests her voice.*

EMMOTT. Rowland Torre, I do love you!!!

*She listens to it echo.*

ROWLAND. Shhh, the sound it travels!

EMMOTT. I do not care. Rowland Torre, I do love you!

ROWLAND. We will be found. Come down.

EMMOTT. Only if you do promise to kiss me.

ROWLAND. Alright.

EMMOTT. '*Alright*'? You do have a way with words, Rowland.

ROWLAND *drags* EMMOTT *down onto the floor. They kiss.*

Forget the reverend. Forget Eyam. Forget this world we know. We shall start anew. There shall never be walls or boundaries. We will make our own future.

ROWLAND. Yes.

EMMOTT. I love you.

EMMOTT *and* ROWLAND *kiss.*

Now your turn. Rowland!

ROWLAND....Emmott Sydall, I... do love yer.

EMMOTT. That were pathetic. Heard you speak more passionate to a loaf of bread.

ROWLAND. Emmott Sydall, I do love yer.

EMMOTT. Again!

ROWLAND. Emmott Sydall, I do love yer!

EMMOTT. Louder!!

ROWLAND. Emmott Sydall, I do love yer!!!

EMMOTT *beams as she runs back to the village, chasing the echo.*

Emmott? Are yer coming back? Later? Later, is it? Alright. She's coming back later…

ROWLAND *exits.*

**7.**

STANLEY *drags Anne's coffin through the village.*

*Exhausted, he rests.*

STANLEY *becomes aware that* WILLIAM *is watching him.*

WILLIAM. Reverend Stanley.

STANLEY. –

WILLIAM. We must speak.

STANLEY. I am burying my wife.

WILLIAM. Can I be of help?

STANLEY. No.

WILLIAM. It is a beautiful spot. Peaceful.

STANLEY. It is what Eyam offered her.

WILLIAM. I can imagine so. And what of you, have you made peace with Eyam?

STANLEY *starts to drag the coffin again.*

The situation is unprecedented, what with your history here.

STANLEY. History?

WILLIAM. My intention is not to erase the past. The world though moves forward, holding on to the past will only cause harm.

STANLEY. What age are you?

WILLIAM. So I can be told you have twice my years, knowledge, experience. I have heard such reasoning by many men before. It is fear that makes men say it. Fear of not knowing what place they inhabit in our new world.

STANLEY. I have lived through change. This outlook; frivolity, excess – it is a phase. A wave passing back then forth, nothing more. A transition, the body cleansing itself of all its bile, a cycle society does regrettably go through.

WILLIAM. You've heard not a single word from any sermon I have led, yet stand there so confident in a belief it is frivolous.

STANLEY. I do not require hear it.

WILLIAM. How very Christian to judge so.

STANLEY. I've seen your like.

WILLIAM. My like?

STANLEY. Gleaming ambition. This is my home. My people. Not a stepping stone. That is all Eyam is to you.

WILLIAM. No.

STANLEY. Skip, skip, then move on to bigger, grander parishes.

WILLIAM. Reverend –

STANLEY. Do not call me by such word! My name is Mr Stanley!

WILLIAM. If this community thou seeks build begins with an individual, it shall always be the one who stands tallest, loudest that will dictate the moral shape you wish to be its lead.

STANLEY. Is there a point you skirt?

WILLIAM. I see that it is noble to offer Sheldon chance to change. For if that man, capable of such vile act, could alter, what greater symbol could there be for a community to follow suit.

STANLEY. Think that is my intent?

WILLIAM. With the most generous benefit of doubt. But it is a failure. A man of our calling. A man of God he did hang from a tree, dragged to death.

STANLEY. Many were there.

WILLIAM. That is not something to praise! Are you immersed so deep in role of puppet you no longer feel the arm that manipulates?

STANLEY. I am no puppet!

WILLIAM. Who pays for your stay? Whom? So long as you stay here that is all you are.

STANLEY. I am God's servant.

WILLIAM. God has not brought you to Eyam. He banished you.

STANLEY. This is my home!

WILLIAM. Do not stare at these hills as if they are yours. They are trusted to me, by God!

STANLEY. They are mine!

WILLIAM. I hoped opportunity for unity. Clear now it will never be a hand you do wish shake. It leaves me little option; I shall call upon the law to expel you.

STANLEY. You would see me evicted, arrested, beaten?

WILLIAM. It is the only path left open.

STANLEY. You have not the stomach for it.

WILLIAM. Before arriving here I might have agreed.

STANLEY. Do I scare you so?

WILLIAM. No, *Reverend*. It were pity not fear I once had for the likes of you. But understand, this is my parish.

STANLEY. This village will fall at your hands.

WILLIAM. Attend your wife, I pray the act stirs memory, I am told she was a woman who offered great sense.

WILLIAM *goes*.

STANLEY *stares after him, full of venom. He then begins the task of dragging the coffin to its resting place.*

**8.**

COOPERS' *cottage*. VICCARS *and* EDWARD *are folding cloth. As they do, they gradually get closer and closer.*

VICCARS. Never left Eyam? Not once?

EDWARD. Mother is incapable of travel. Think I can leave her by herself?

VICCARS. I do. She is capable, Edward. Plenty capable.

EDWARD. I would not know where to begin.

VICCARS *watches* EDWARD.

Is it true that dogs the size of cows roam waiting to devour those who stray from the road?

VICCARS. Did your mother tell you that? No, Edward. Or whatever other myths she has spun.

EDWARD. If I could see but one thing, what should it be? What would you take me to see?

VICCARS. What would I have you see...?

EDWARD....I do mean... I...

*They are so close.* MARY COOPER *enters.*

MARY COOPER. It won't intrude. Those words came from your mouth.

EDWARD. Mother, it is only cloth we fold. Not assemble a suit.

MARY COOPER. Ha! What do you know of clothes and thread? Do you know only recently I have had to dress him. The shame. At his age. It is not a task fitting for a mother.

EDWARD. Mother.

MARY COOPER. He will deny it, it is what spineless boys do.

*A knock at the door.* MARY COOPER *goes to the door.*

Never any peace in this house. Mrs Sheldon? What does that money-grabbing little whore care for?

EDWARD. Open. Do not keep her waiting.

MARY COOPER. Oh, to hell with her. She were born in just as much shit as the rest of us, however hard she washes, smell never leaves.

MARY COOPER *opens the door to* ELIZABETH SHELDON.

Mrs Sheldon, welcome! This is an honour.

ELIZABETH SHELDON. Evening. I was told a tailor lived here.

MARY COOPER. Yes, my lodger. Mr Viccars. Him.

VICCARS. Mrs Cooper, I have not solicited this.

MARY COOPER. Save your words. This will be discussed later.

MARY COOPER *steps aside as* VICCARS *goes to the door.*

VICCARS. Good evening.

ELIZABETH SHELDON. Hello. I have never known a tailor in Eyam before.

VICCARS. Not for years I am told.

ELIZABETH SHELDON. Ah, they talk to you.

VICCARS. How can I assist?

ELIZABETH SHELDON. May I see your hands?

VICCARS *shows his hands.*

Never broken a rock before, have you?

VICCARS. I have never broken a rock.

ELIZABETH SHELDON. So soft. We could be sisters. Are you skilled?

VICCARS. Yes.

*She laughs.*

ELIZABETH SHELDON. You would be a poor salesman if you said no. But you are skilled, aren't you?

VICCARS. Yes.

ELIZABETH SHELDON. I require a dress.

VICCARS. Tell me what you wish from this dress. Is it for a ball, for daywear?

ELIZABETH SHELDON. I wish for a dress that a man could admire as much in its fitting as in the desire to remove. To wear it would bring an end to being by oneself. It would bring a child. Wearing it would be a means of escape. Could you make such a dress? Say you could.

VICCARS. I could.

ELIZABETH SHELDON. Thank you.

VICCARS. But I must order materials. A dress such as this requires fabric not available here.

ELIZABETH SHELDON. Then I will trust you to do that. This will cover the material?

VICCARS. That is more than plenty.

ELIZABETH SHELDON. Then the rest shall be an advance.

*A moment.*

Do you wish to measure me? We could do so now.

MARY COOPER *coughs.*

VICCARS. When the material arrives.

ELIZABETH SHELDON. I shall return then.

MARY COOPER *coughs.*

VICCARS. When it arrives I shall come to your home and take measurements.

ELIZABETH SHELDON. It must remain our secret. My husband for him it must be a surprise.

VICCARS. Secrets I have never struggled to keep.

ELIZABETH SHELDON. Do you think my husband will like it?

MARY COOPER *has had enough.*

MARY COOPER. Mrs Sheldon, Mr Sheldon must be wondering where you are. Heaven forbid he thinks we've held you prisoner!

ELIZABETH SHELDON. Yes, I should return. Good day.

VICCARS. Good day.

> ELIZABETH SHELDON *leaves*.

I do not know where she lives.

EDWARD. It is not hard to find.

MARY COOPER. I should have had a daughter. A beautiful daughter, one I could marry off. To a rich man. Then I wouldn't have to live like this.

VICCARS. I will tidy this now.

MARY COOPER. Yes, you will.

EDWARD. Mother!

MARY COOPER. And now he raises his voice at his own mother. God, how have I wronged thee, for this to be my life? How?

VICCARS. Edward. Hadrian's Wall.

MARY COOPER. What's that? Why are you smiling?

EDWARD. Your cloth, Mr Viccars. Mother, I'm going for a walk.

MARY COOPER. A walk? What are you, a dog? Did you not hear me? Edward? Answer me?

> EDWARD *exits*. VICCARS *goes to his room*. MARY COOPER *is left by herself*.

**9.**

*Eyam Church.* WILLIAM *is at the pulpit.*

WILLIAM. I stand here before you a stranger.
    Tradition implies I be hesitant
    Time, after all, is required for trust to build.
    Yet I look out upon all gathered and all I feel is awe.
    For such generosity is shown.
    From every face I feel warmth.
    Love is clear the vehicle that brings us here.
    …No. No. No, William, they hung your predecessor that is
    not love…

HOWE. Finished?

WILLIAM. Howe? I was practising. Have you been here all the
    time?

HOWE. Sadly. Some say it's a sign of madness, talking to
    yerself.

WILLIAM. People such as yourself?

HOWE. Yes.

WILLIAM. Howe, I cannot do it, cannot keep the pretence!
    This talk of love and warmth, these people, none attend.
    How long must I continue this act? Near a month but we
    bare have a congregation.

HOWE. Give 'em time.

WILLIAM. How much, though?

HOWE. More.

WILLIAM. So long as that non-conformist…! Stanley stays, or
    Sheldon holds his grip, is that how long?

HOWE. Maybe. Me dinner's getting cold.

WILLIAM. Yes, yes, your dinner, of course. Howe, does it
    mark a man weak if he cannot resolve quarrel with words?
    Before arrival here I thought the answer yes. Now though,
    I waver. You see, to see all that inhabits this glorious earth:
    from gulls that glide above the cliffs, to a plant that thrives in
    most hostile climate – it is apparent life adapts to where it

inhabits. And that is the task I am faced with now, is it not? For it is I that must change not as I thought my environment. And Eyam is a village shaped by action.

HOWE. Leave yer to lock up then.

HOWE *goes*.

WILLIAM *is left alone*.

*A crow cries, he stares at it. Another appears. Flanking him.*

WILLIAM *shudders. Exits*.

**10.**

COOPERS' *cottage*. EDWARD *waits*. VICCARS *returns*. EDWARD *gestures for silence*.

EDWARD. Mother's sleeping.

VICCARS *approaches* EDWARD.

She may wake at any moment.

VICCARS. Edward.

EDWARD *steps away from* VICCARS *and retrieves a parcel*.

EDWARD. This did arrive for you. I kept hidden from Mother. Will it be the cloth for Mrs Sheldon?

VICCARS. It will be.

EDWARD. Should we not open it?

VICCARS. Edward, it can wait.

EDWARD. She is not a lady to disappoint.

VICCARS. I wish to talk to you.

EDWARD. Mr Viccars, please.

VICCARS. George…

EDWARD *opens the packet. He unfolds the fabric.*

EDWARD. It is damp. The fabric.

VICCARS. Leave it be.

EDWARD. Mrs Sheldon paid you in good faith.

VICCARS. Let us place it by the fire.

*They hang the cloth.*

What scares you?

EDWARD. How can you ask that? Is this why you live as you do? Town to town? No family to call on? No God?

VICCARS. I was never more alone than when I had them.

*VICCARS comes closer.*

I will complete this then I will leave. Edward, there will be more than enough money. More than enough, Edward.

EDWARD. George…

VICCARS. This is not a cage, Edward. There is a door. Follow me through.

*They hold each other.*

*A gust of wind catches the cloth.*

*It flies through the village.*

*Song.*

VICCARS *unbuttons his shirt.*

*He is covered in boils.*

VICCARS *dies.*

EDWARD *holds him.*

*Crows descend.*

*Crows cry.*

*A howl of despair.*

*Crows scatter.*

**11.**

*Outside* COOPERS' *cottage.*

*A crowd is gathered.*

HOWE. Dead, beyond dead, very long time dead too. Mary, the Lord only knows how you'd not come to notice a rotten carcass in yer house.

MARY COOPER. Edward told me Viccars had left. I had his rent, what cause had I to check?

HOWE. Fact it smelt worse than a badger's arse.

HARRIET. Murdered him.

MARY COOPER. My son is no murderer.

UNWIN. Girl makes a good point, why else would he say the tailor left?

HARRIET. Guilty as sin!

STANLEY. Do not turn to gossip. A man is dead. Pay respect.

HOWE. There is something odd about that boy. Sits, growling, guarding the stinking bed.

STANLEY. Bring the body out.

HOWE. I'll need a hand. This heat, there's been some decay – he's not stiff.

HARRIET. Me, me!

> HARRIET *disappears into the house.* WILLIAM *and* KATHERINE *arrive.*

HOWE. Only a month f'yer first corpse. Not bad going, Reverend.

KATHERINE. Who?

HOWE. The tailor. Though to look upon would not think he once were human.

WILLIAM. Who summoned you?

STANLEY. I did. A man lies dead. He could not be left to rot.

HARRIET *rushes out of the house and vomits.*

HARRIET. Howe, hurry up, dead people can't move themselves!

HARRIET *races back in.* HOWE *follows her.*

WILLIAM. This is not your role.

STANLEY. Many days the man laid in state of neglect. Would you have me leave him to decay without no prayer?

WILLIAM. I had not been informed.

STANLEY. Mary, did you seek out this man?

MARY COOPER. I did not. I came to you.

WILLIAM. Mary, it is I you should have called upon.

MARY COOPER. By that account if I were in need of guidance, prayer, I should come to you as well.

WILLIAM. Yes. Those duties are my responsibility.

EMMOTT *enters.* ELIZABETH SYDALL *stops her.*

EMMOTT. What's happened?

ELIZABETH SYDALL. Wait, Emmott. The tailor is dead.

HOWE *and* HARRIET *exit the cottage carrying the corpse in a blanket. A distraught* EDWARD *follows close behind.*

HARRIET. It stinks in there!

EDWARD. Mother? Mother, where are they taking him?!

HOWE. Mary, control the boy.

MARY COOPER. Step away, Edward.

EMMOTT. Edward, come away.

EMMOTT *takes* EDWARD *and attempts to drag him away.* ELIZABETH SYDALL *and* KATHERINE *come and help.*

KATHERINE. They take him to be buried, Edward.

EDWARD. I have not said goodbye. Let me hold him.

EMMOTT. Unwin, give us a hand!

UNWIN. Fuck that!

MARY COOPER. Edward, stop making a scene. He is only dead.

EDWARD *breaks free from those holding him.*

EDWARD. Because of me! Because of what I am!! This is my punishment!!!

MARY COOPER. Enough boy. Inside now! Inside!!

MARY COOPER, EMMOTT *and* ELIZABETH SYDALL *drag a wailing* EDWARD *inside.*

STANLEY. Howe, follow me. I will see him buried.

WILLIAM. You will do no such thing. Howe, I am to attend, to bury.

STANLEY. No man deserves your words for their last.

WILLIAM. Release your grip.

HARRIET. Cor, they're going to fight!

KATHERINE. They are not going to fight.

HOWE. They are.

WILLIAM. Stand back, Reverend Stanley. Stand back!

KATHERINE. William!

*They struggle, fight over the corpse. To the encouragement/ dismay of the village. They drop the body. The sheets open. The body rolls out. Rotten. Flies escape. Everyone recoils at the smell.* STANLEY *steps well away.* HARRIET *dry heaves,* UNWIN *vomits.*

HARRIET. Flies! Hundreds of flies!!

WILLIAM. God forgive me, what have I done?

UNWIN. What sins this man committed, pure wickedness escapes his body.

UNWIN *exits.*

HOWE. There, now perhaps all will see what tasks I endure. Not squabble when I ask for raise.

STANLEY. Be ashamed, Mompesson – this is upon you. Never before have I been driven to such acts.

STANLEY *goes*.

HOWE. Away, all of yer.

*All bar* HARRIET, HOWE, KATHERINE *and* WILLIAM *exit*.

HARRIET. Er, what are them all over his body?

HOWE. Away, girl. Away.

HARRIET *goes*.

KATHERINE. Must wrap him up before the flies do worse.

WILLIAM. I will assist.

HOWE. You have assisted plenty enough, Reverend.

HOWE *covers* VICCARS' *body*.

*Song*.

## 12.

*A sparse funeral*.

EDWARD *watches on*.

HOWE *starts to whistle as the body is buried*.

MARY COOPER *drags* EDWARD *away*.

*Till only* HOWE, *who continues to shovel soil*, WILLIAM *and* KATHERINE *remain*.

WILLIAM. Howe, please, a word. What talk is there of Mr Viccars' death?

HOWE. Yer mean the boils, lesions –

KATHERINE. None here is a physician.

HOWE. We all saw what we saw. There is no talk. Bar the ghoul and Cooper boy, none cared about him enough to look.

WILLIAM. You have told no other of the marks?

HOWE. I'm a sheep, not a shepherd.

WILLIAM. To commit to it being... that... would create panic, a tide I feel would be hard to stop.

HOWE. I don't fear it. In this job yer build a wall between yerself and death. But not all others have that, lot have yet to make their peace with God.

WILLIAM. It has been two days, yet nothing more, no others have shown symptoms.

HOWE. None that have required my assistance.

KATHERINE. Pray that God keep all safe.

HOWE. Aye, if not, I'll need a new shovel. Reverend, so yer know, Stanley never talked to me: I felt safer f'that.

*Song builds.*

## 13.

EDWARD *wears* ELIZABETH SHELDON's *dress. It is magnificent. He admires its craft and then starts to dance. He strips his clothes. He is covered in boils. He continues to dance, wilder and wilder. Finally free.*

**14.**

MARY COOPER. Reverend?! Reverend?!!

*Rectory.* WILLIAM.

Reverend, what evil I must have done?!! It is my idle, vicious tongue. I am a sinner, it is the only answer!!

WILLIAM. Mary, what is this talk?

MARY COOPER. Get you out!!!

MARY COOPER *screams and starts to claw at her tongue.*

WILLIAM. Mary, stop, stop this!

MARY COOPER....Reverend, he is gone.

WILLIAM. Gone?

MARY COOPER. It takes him from me, Reverend. It takes him from me. My boy!

KATHERINE *enters.*

WILLIAM. Lord help us.

KATHERINE. What is it, William?

WILLIAM. The plague is here.

*Screams.*

**15.**

*Village.* SYDALLS' *cottage. Chaos, as* ELIZABETH SYDALL *appears at her door.*

UNWIN. Elizabeth! Elizabeth, do not step out of your door!

ELIZABETH SYDALL. John?! John!!

UNWIN. She means to spread it.

JOHN WILSON. Stand back, stand back!

UNWIN. John, if you walk to her you do not walk back.

> JOHN WILSON *forces his way through to* ELIZABETH SYDALL.

JOHN WILSON. Elizabeth?

ELIZABETH SYDALL. Emily is gone.

UNWIN. It jumps from house to house. We will be next.

HOWE. Elizabeth, best you return within.

JOHN WILSON. Let her mourn!

STANLEY. Emily is with God now.

ELIZABETH SYDALL. God! She were seven years old.

STANLEY. Place trust in God, this is his path for sweet Emily.

JOHN WILSON. Those words are not the comfort required.

STANLEY. All must look within as to why this arrives. Punishment. Frivolity, adultery, covetousness, sodemy, greed, all have lived here. Acceptance is now what you must ask for.

JOHN WILSON. I pray you showed your Anne more comfort on her depart.

> WILLIAM *and* KATHERINE *arrive.*

WILLIAM. What's happened?

JOHN WILSON. Emily is gone.

WILLIAM. Where is your husband, Elizabeth?

ELIZABETH SYDALL. Within. He refuses to let her go.

HOWE. Best leave this to me.

HARRIET. I want to see the dead baby!

HARRIET *goes into the house followed by* HOWE. JOHN
HANCOCK *enters.*

ELIZABETH SYDALL. She fell so quick.

WILLIAM. Did you hold her?

ELIZABETH SYDALL *nods.*

All here, return to your houses, turn your thoughts to prayer.

UNWIN. Forget prayer, load bags.

WILLIAM. Unwin, wait. Wait!

JOHN HANCOCK. You shall not do that.

UNWIN. Or what?

WILLIAM. You will let me attend to those /

UNWIN. Every second you speak is a wasted second.

WILLIAM. / whose grief requires me. Let me be heard, man!

UNWIN. Could be miles gone!

JOHN HANCOCK. Quiet.

STANLEY. Did you know of this, Reverend?

WILLIAM. All know that people have died.

STANLEY. But you knew it were the plague.

WILLIAM. There were signs.

JOHN WILSON. You knew?!

UNWIN. Yer what?!

STANLEY. And he kept it secret!

JOHN HANCOCK. Is this true?

UNWIN. You lying Yorkshire bastard.

UNWIN *has gone.*

WILLIAM. He placed me in an impossible situation!

STANLEY. You attempt place fault at my door?

WILLIAM. Whole village attempted to set against me. I had to be certain in face of such reception.

STANLEY. Why do you think the sickness here, Reverend?

WILLIAM. I don't seek to know that answer.

STANLEY. Nothing exists for no reason. This is a message from God.

KATHERINE. Then he sends it as our challenge.

STANLEY. Challenge? No, it is you, your decadent ways that bring this. Finally we are to be cleansed. God has returned to Eyam.

EMMOTT *runs to her mother.* KATHERINE *intercepts her.*

EMMOTT. Mother? Mother?!

KATHERINE. Emmott, stay back.

JOHN HANCOCK. Emmott, it is in your house. Emily is gone.

JOHN SYDALL *exits his house carrying his dead daughter.* HOWE *follows him.*

HOWE. Madness. Won't put her down.

JOHN SYDALL. You! This should be you!

ELIZABETH SYDALL. John, do not say such a thing!

JOHN SYDALL. She brought shame into this house. This is holy vengeance. Is it not, Mr Stanley?

EMMOTT. Wretched man!

JOHN SYDALL. Even now she speaks ill!

HOWE. Give Emily to me!

JOHN SYDALL. Remove your hands!!

JOHN SYDALL *suddenly coughs. He staggers,* HOWE *takes the body from him. People move away from* JOHN SYDALL.

What?

JOHN WILSON. Go inside, Sydall.

JOHN SYDALL. Now it strikes me.

EMMOTT. God does exist.

JOHN SYDALL. Is this what you wish? This upon me?

JOHN SYDALL *tries to go towards* EMMOTT.

Poisoned slut!

JOHN WILSON *punches* JOHN SYDALL. JOHN SYDALL *lies on the floor.*

This is how you always saw it, Wilson? Me dead? At last, all those years spent dreaming of snaking your way up into my wife's clam.

JOHN HANCOCK. Inside, John.

STANLEY. Do as he says.

JOHN SYDALL. I thought you here to save, instead you bring the end.

STANLEY. May God grant you peace.

JOHN SYDALL. Peace? Who cares for peace? May you all burn in hell!

JOHN SYDALL *steps back inside.*

HOWE. I'll dig her a nice hole. Deep enough even the foxes won't touch.

HOWE *carries the body away. He whistles as he does.* HARRIET *follows, she also whistles, but it is sinister.*

JOHN HANCOCK. Emmott, where do you go?

EMMOTT. I must warn Rowland. You should warn your family.

EMMOTT *exits as* JOHN HANCOCK *heads in the opposite direction.*

JOHN WILSON. Elizabeth?

ELIZABETH SYDALL. I must go back within.

ELIZABETH SYDALL *walks back into the house.*

JOHN WILSON. I shall never hold my baby.

JOHN WILSON *walks away. Leaving* WILLIAM,
KATHERINE *and* STANLEY.

STANLEY. For too long I have stood idle. With you here, your
weakness, all are vulnerable. I must act, take matters into my
own hands.

WILLIAM. What does that mean?

STANLEY. It means enough, I shall lead.

STANLEY *exits*.

WILLIAM. This is not your village!

KATHERINE. William.

WILLIAM. Could he be right? We arrive, then this.

KATHERINE. No, William.

WILLIAM. If this be God's will, the sickness can go no further
than the walls Eyam has created.

KATHERINE. Agreed.

WILLIAM. Katherine, you must leave Eyam now.

KATHERINE. William? You cannot ask for what you yourself
cannot stand by.

WILLIAM. I promised in God's name to keep you safe.

KATHERINE. If we are all to fall it must be as equals. I will
not leave your side, William.

WILLIAM. I implore.

KATHERINE. No.

WILLIAM. Katherine –

KATHERINE. This is not your decision, it is mine.

WILLIAM. The children.

KATHERINE. It is only through unity that we save them. You
questioned why we were sent here, why we kept our dearest
loves behind: now God shows the reason.

WILLIAM. May God in his wisdom have mercy upon us.

## 16.

*The Delph.* EMMOTT *and* ROWLAND. *A great distance separates them.*

EMMOTT. Mercy, what is mercy? Sweet dearest Emily, Rowland, her face were distorted so violent. Stolen from us. Mercy is a myth.

ROWLAND. Emmott.

EMMOTT. Rowland, not a foot further! Hear me?! You cannot come close to me.

ROWLAND. But we are to leave together?

EMMOTT. That dream is to bed now. Father coughs already. His fate sealed. No angel will mark his passing.

ROWLAND. It is in your house. You cannot return.

EMMOTT. It may be too late already.

ROWLAND. No. You are well.

EMMOTT. Would it be your family's home we run to?

ROWLAND. At first. Then –

EMMOTT. I do not ask for the story, Rowland. Do you not see? I may already be afflicted. I cannot be the person who spreads... your sister, your mother. No, I will not.

ROWLAND. Then I shall cross the line. I shall join you in Eyam.

EMMOTT. Stay there.

ROWLAND. I love you.

EMMOTT. If you love me you will stay there.

ROWLAND. I cannot leave you.

EMMOTT. All these words, the declarations – prove it. I will not have your death on my hands. If you truly love me, you will listen to me when I say you will not step foot in this village until told it is safe. Not a second before.

ROWLAND. Emmott –

EMMOTT. Do you love me?

ROWLAND. I do.

EMMOTT. Then it is agreed.

ROWLAND. I cannot even hold you?

EMMOTT. This is not goodbye. Here, this spot, over this ridge, through trees, under the sky, our words will meet and keep our love alive.

**17.**

SHELDONS' *gardens*. FRANCIS *is carrying* SHELDON*'s cases*. STANLEY *approaches*.

STANLEY. Francis, what is this?

FRANCIS. I f-fol-follow instru-ction is all.

*The* SHELDONS *approach*.

ELIZABETH SHELDON. Francis, we do not employ you as a statue!

SHELDON. Ah, Thomas, certain if you ask nice we can find space within the carriage.

STANLEY. You mean to flee?

SHELDON. Flee is a dramatic term. A *mosey* elsewhere. The world does not end at this parish's borders, Thomas. It is time we paid visit to our other homes, friends, family.

STANLEY. Another is dead.

FRANCIS. Who-who-who is dead?

SHELDON. Never you mind, Francis.

STANLEY. Emily Sydall. Only seven. Her father not far behind.

FRANCIS. Sw-sweet mercy.

STANLEY. It is time to stand by each other.

SHELDON. To unite as one? No one in, no one out?

STANLEY. Aye.

SHELDON. Oh, Thomas, even a fool knows that will not work. All here are like a pack of dogs fighting over a bone.

STANLEY. Prove them wrong. Stay. Together we will lead.

SHELDON. Ah togetherness, how noble. It does only work though if you have nothing to lose.

STANLEY. People will lose their lives to follow that belief.

SHELDON. What lives? Scrimping, living in filth. No wonder they would eat your words up.

STANLEY. I thought you a man lost. In search of guidance, direction.

SHELDON. Only direction I seek is the exit.

STANLEY. I have lain with the devil!

ELIZABETH SHELDON. Francis, hurry!

FRANCIS. People w-wi-will not... flee?

STANLEY. Those who do defy God.

FRANCIS *drops the bags. Goes and stands with* STANLEY.

SHELDON. Where's the 'fuck you', Francis?

FRANCIS. It's up-up your ar-arse.

STANLEY. After all you have done to make Eyam yours. The people quashed, land grabbed, yet you run –

SHELDON. Thomas, the deeds are mine, I take Eyam wherever I go.

STANLEY. All will know what choice you made.

SHELDON. History is written by the survivors.

STANLEY. And the cowards.

SHELDON. Elizabeth, why hesitate, get on board. Wife, what do you think will happen here? Oh, how luminous your skin is. /

ELIZABETH SHELDON. Stop.

SHELDON. You've heard stories from London of what the plague brings. How it rots the skin /

ELIZABETH SHELDON. Stop.

SHELDON. / flesh does melt. Beauty eaten from within. /

ELIZABETH SHELDON. Stop.

STANLEY. Mrs Sheldon, you have family in Tideswell. /

ELIZABETH SHELDON. Stop.

SHELDON. / Death is all that what waits for us here.

STANLEY. / These people you intend leave will die to keep your family safe.

ELIZABETH SHELDON. I said stop!

SHELDON. Think those in Eyam or Tideswell care for you? Darling, they despise you. That's one thing about animals: once you've left the pack they never let you return. This is your life now.

STANLEY. Mrs Sheldon, the first man who succumbed, George Viccars, you may know him as a tailor. He placed order for a fine linen, a linen only found in London. That linen was for you.

ELIZABETH SHELDON. Try to lay this blame with me?

STANLEY. A frivolous expense. /

ELIZABETH SHELDON. No. No. No.

STANLEY. / That no others here could ever even dream.

ELIZABETH SHELDON. You think God entrusts you to speak such words in His name?

STANLEY. Know it is the truth. Redeem yourself.

ELIZABETH SHELDON. Look to your own failings before casting blame further afield.

STANLEY. Praise God, the Moseley name was taken from you.

*A dagger blow.* ELIZABETH SHELDON *exits.*

SHELDON. Next time our paths cross, Stanley, it will be me dancing on your grave.

*SHELDON exits, carrying what he can. STANLEY watches on.*

FRANCIS. Mr Stanley, what-what are we to do?

*Bells ring in the distance.*

STANLEY. Come, Francis, our job is not yet done.

*They exit.*

**18.**

*Bells continue to ring.*

*The village is chaotically assembling around the green.*

UNWIN. See it's started! Sheldon has fled.

MARY TALBOT. He is rich, the rich always look after themselves first.

UNWIN. Well, I want to be rich!

MARY TALBOT. Well yer not. None of us here are. But poverty should not be our trap. It should be pride that keeps us. We go elsewhere, we'll never be free. It is better to die a free man than a slave.

UNWIN. Fuck dying. It ain't on my to-do list!

HARRIET. Nor mine!

*KATHERINE and WILLIAM approach.*

MARY TALBOT. Reverend, we meet as you asked, but for how long it cannot be guaranteed.

*The HANCOCKS and FRANCIS have now entered. STANLEY soon after, yet he remains watching.*

WILLIAM. We gather here amidst a storm, a storm that feeds, grows with every moment. It wraps itself within and chills us till our bones rattle.

UNWIN. Enough of the prose!

WILLIAM. I was sent here to provide stability. Time has not been the friend I hoped it would, still much to do, many rifts to heal and –

UNWIN. You'd all die listening to that? He's not even from Derbyshire.

WILLIAM. Yes, I was not born here amongst you. To many I am still a stranger. But I know that here there is decentness. A community. Together we can unite.

UNWIN. Together!

FRANCIS. T-to-together, yes!

UNWIN. Shut up, Francis.

FRANCIS. No. No. NO. I, I was given option to leave with Shel-Sheldon, but, but have stayed, Unwin.

UNWIN. Well, you've always been a fucking fool.

HARRIET. Ha-ha, fool, you're going to die. You'll g-g-get the plague.

HOWE. Enough, girl.

UNWIN. I only say what all are thinking.

JOHN HANCOCK. What do you want from us, Reverend?

UNWIN. He wants us to die.

WILLIAM. No, to live –

UNWIN. Thinks we're fools!

MARY TALBOT. Let the reverend speak!

UNWIN. Speak? Every second here is a waste when we could be on our way.

MARY TALBOT. And where would yer go, Unwin? Yer struggle to find a welcome here, let alone when tarred with being from a village rife with plague.

UNWIN. Joke, but I need no friends, no welcome. I mek me own way. Look at them next t'yer, d'yer trust 'em?

HOWE. No.

UNWIN. See!

HOWE. But if I were stood over there by Mary or John or anyone but you.

JOHN HANCOCK. I've fought enough to stay on my land, I ain't giving up now.

UNWIN. Oh, here we go again. You and fighting for yer bloody land. Not a blade of grass you've not bored with that tale, John. Well, yer may a won the battle but yer lost the war.

ELIZABETH HANCOCK (*to* JOHN HANCOCK). Is this not the final straw? Finally, we can start again.

JOHN HANCOCK. No, Elizabeth.

UNWIN. Own wife wants out, John!

ELIZABETH HANCOCK. What good is land if we're all dead? Young ones like Harriet, they deserve a chance, John.

HARRIET. Heh, you don't speak for me! I'm staying. There's going to be so many bodies to play with!

ELIZABETH HANCOCK. Mary, please speak sense to him.

MARY TALBOT. I'd rather be buried by my worse enemy than a stranger.

MARY COOPER *enters, bedraggled, lost.*

UNWIN. Mary Cooper, you've got nothing left to stay here for.

MARY COOPER. Oh my little boy, my boy is dead!

UNWIN. Aye, he's as rotten as an apple fallen in winter.

MARY COOPER. Edward always wanted to see beyond Eyam. Howe – to his grave – he will be dug up, I will fulfill his wishes!

HARRIET. Cor!

MARY TALBOT. Grief talking, Mary.

HOWE. He stays where he lays.

MARY COOPER. All should feel my pain!

MARY TALBOT *slaps* MARY COOPER.

MARY TALBOT. Dammit, woman. Edward were a gentle boy – do not hijack his soul with madness.

ELIZABETH HANCOCK. This is a vision with only death as its outcome. Stay is suicide. Is there not no greater sin in God's eyes?

EMMOTT. Want to be the person who spreads it, do you, Elizabeth? Want that to be how you're known? Run, that's your risk.

JOHN HANCOCK. She's not running.

EMMOTT. The one who took not her own but the lives of those in Stoney Middleton, Tideswell, your son Thomas in Sheffield.

UNWIN. Ignore her: she, she's had the sense fucked out of her, she will be gone to that baker's any moment.

*Chaos.* EMMOTT *tries to attack* UNWIN. JOHN WILSON *ends up holding her back.*

JOHN WILSON. Watch your mouth.

EMMOTT. There is nothing I'd wish more than to be with him! /

UNWIN. Hear her, true all know it!

EMMOTT. / But I am still here!

KATHERINE. Enough!

EMMOTT. I will not be the person who risks others. I believe in love. In unity. That is the future I want. Give us that and I will stay.

HARRIET. I'm going to marry Rowland when yer dead.

EMMOTT. Then I will haunt your every step.

HARRIET. Cor, my own ghost!

UNWIN. All this talk is for the weak and fools. I speak only the truth.

KATHERINE. Talk of truth? Then hear this: survival, that word you seek, life, well, it is only possible together.

UNWIN. Together!

KATHERINE. Yes, together. That is strength not weakness.

JOHN WILSON. It is easy for you to say, your children are safe.

KATHERINE. Safe yes, but I accept that I may never hold them again.

JOHN WILSON. To even have that.

MARY COOPER. John, you've knocked up a married woman, I'd ease up on the judgement!

MARY TALBOT. Didn't take long for yer to be back to yerself, Mary.

FRANCIS. Could we-could we? We could go to the w-woods. Spread a-f-far. Prox-proximity is pestilen-lence fr-friend –

UNWIN, MARY COOPER, ELIZABETH HANCOCK *and* HARRIET. Francis, shut up!

MARY TALBOT. Reverend, why are you not speaking? Give us your plan. Plainly.

WILLIAM. A quarantine.

UNWIN. A what?!

WILLIAM. No one in. No one out. Till sufficient time between loss of life has passed we know the sickness halted.

JOHN HANCOCK. How long?

WILLIAM.…Two months.

ELIZABETH HANCOCK. Two months?!

WILLIAM. Three?

*Overwhelming chorus of disapproval. From the practical 'What will we live on' (*JOHN WILSON*), to the ridiculous 'I've had piles that have lasted less time' (*UNWIN*), to the blunt truth 'I will not do it, John' (*ELIZABETH HANCOCK*).*

A month.

UNWIN. What month? 'Ave yer ever lived through January –
it goes on forever!

HOWE. He means length of time not specific month, idiot.

ELIZABETH HANCOCK. Then say it clearly.

KATHERINE. Twenty-eight days.

UNWIN. Twenty-eight days?

WILLIAM. Yes. Twenty-eight days.

UNWIN. But –

MARY TALBOT. You'll be fine, Unwin, you'll be able to count
it down on all yer fingers and toes.

UNWIN. Not even Mr Stanley will stand beside yer.

STANLEY. May God never hear what I have heard said here.
For I am ashamed.

UNWIN. What they ask is vast.

STANLEY. Is it vast to ask you to show faith? To conquer fear?
If the thought of death scares you, then God is not in your
heart. If God wants us dead, He wants us dead. And to die
committing to this act would be a blessing. Do you love God?

UNWIN. I do.

STANLEY (*to the rest*). Do you?

*The others agree, bar* HARRIET *who shrugs.*

Then you have no need to fear death. Speak to them.

WILLIAM. Eyam sits on a hill, forever looking out, but is it not
time to alter and to look within?

WILLIAM *senses he may have lost the village.*

Could we not be where others look to for courage,
inspiration?
Make no mistake, we have a chance to halt this sickness at
its root.
That is within our power.
It is our choice.

What I suggest I know will not be easy.

I am not asking you to walk blindly.

Look around you.

Husbands, wives, daughters, sons, neighbours, even those you thought you would never miss.

Many will not fill the space they stand in now.

Lives will be lost.

Many, many lives.

Summer will be our enemy.

We will pray for cold winters and winds that chill the soul.

But do this and we embark on something bigger than ourselves.

A true purpose.

Together, we can show the true beauty of humanity.

Now I ask you, will you stand together?

*They listen. And then slowly, starting with* MARY COOPER, *they start to sing. It is the beginning of something new. A community.*

**PART TWO**

**19.**

*A flock of crows circle.*

*A cacophony of noise as they swoop and cry.*

*They eventually tire.*

KATHERINE. Here the world orbits on the most minuscule
of axis.

Peripheries never having had cause to expand.

A village, perhaps two, some may have seen.

Otherwise where their eyes stop to them does mark the end
of earth.

Yet, still this minute world it shrinks.

Doors stay shut.

Paths and fields lay untrod.

Outside is death.

Ferocious in its hunger.

October steals twenty-three of our populate.

Two families fall quicker than the autumn leaves.

Sydall and Thorpe.

What was once a combined sixteen now stands at five.

Yet still none look to flee.

Twenty-eight days is set as a marker.

When that length passes with no loss all know they shall
be free.

Days become countdowns not accumulate of the month they
occupy.

Six days in November pass without a loss.

But then we begin again.

Four.

Then three.

Eight whole days managed before Christmas arrives.

At home William and I cheer ourselves in memories,

not futures, a fault too late now to rectify,

superstition, as if to start to talk in such a way would
guarantee our own demise.

So stories of the past are what propel us on.
Neither of us correcting when clear it was not how it were.
Birds no longer haunt my dreams, instead they follow our
every step.
Aware we are those who offer prayers to those soon to
become their feast.
Now we welcome in a new year, if welcome is the word.
For I fear it is not the bringing of something new
But the beginning of the end.

## 20.

*Churchyard. Snowfall. The snow begins to form on the ground.*
*WILLIAM watches the flakes fall. Catches a flake, smiles.*
*HOWE joins him, carrying his shovel. Looks up at the sky.*

HOWE. He listens then.

WILLIAM. Pray, let this snow never end.

HOWE. Every inch of ground frozen. Take weeks to thaw.
    Should have dug extra graves in advance.

WILLIAM. Every death we must believe is the last.

HOWE. Easy f'you to say, I dig the holes.

WILLIAM. Ten days have passed, Howe. Ten days.

HOWE. Still got eighteen more.

WILLIAM. For first time in three months we have respite.

HOWE. Don't let snow make yer giddy. Forty-seven of our
    number I've buried, respite is not enough. Finality.

WILLIAM. Forty-seven.

   *Shows notch on his shovel.*

   Must you keep such maudlin record.

HOWE. Size of notches I make reckon a can fit up to hundred-
    fifty.

WILLIAM. That's half the village.

HOWE *nods. They stare at the snow.*

Keep falling.

HOWE. Aye.

KATHERINE *approaches.*

Still plan for a service?

WILLIAM *nods.*

I'll clear path.

HOWE *goes.*

KATHERINE. I come from Old John Thornley.

WILLIAM. Not another?

KATHERINE. No, something new. The cold, William. It is both friend and foe. The man refuses to burn wood to warm his home. I found him his face almost blue, huddled in a blanket, such is his fear of feeding the pestilence.

WILLIAM. I gave instruction to make fire.

KATHERINE. For all good it did. I knocked on more doors, each time met with rooms filled with icy breath. Not a single chimney pours smoke in the air.

WILLIAM. This is Stanley. It is his talk of endurance they hear.

KATHERINE. Reach out to him.

WILLIAM. I will not bow down before that heretic.

KATHERINE. God opposes the proud but shows favour to the humble.

WILLIAM. This is not pride. He is a petulant man. Only yesterday he tells me that he should be given use of the church to lead service. /

KATHERINE. I am well aware.

WILLIAM. / That many in the village do not see my words sufficient. He still takes every moment to undermine what I, we, do.

STANLEY *enters*.

KATHERINE. Mr Stanley. Snow still falls.

STANLEY. It does. Thought more on the village's request?

WILLIAM. It were not the village's request. The answer remains the same.

KATHERINE. William!

STANLEY. I will make all aware of your position. Know they grow restless.

WILLIAM. Restless, ha, at least that keeps them warm – they freeze at your behest.

KATHERINE. Mr Stanley, pray a gentle word. On your visits, what have you said of keeping fires?

STANLEY. We know fires offer breeding for the sickness.

KATHERINE. Cold is taking its place. Many refuse to warm their homes. Elizabeth Sydall eight months pregnant, what way is that for her to live? We must not create another killer. Many feel it is their duty to silently endure.

STANLEY. Endurance is the path to the light.

KATHERINE. Misery is not our savior.

WILLIAM. Tell them to light fires!

STANLEY. Is the madness upon you?

WILLIAM. There is a madness but one of only your making.

KATHERINE. Enough of this. Must you act like children?

STANLEY. I am not a child!

WILLIAM. Nor am I!

*A moment.*

You wish to hold service within?

STANLEY. Know full well.

WILLIAM. Say yes.

STANLEY. Yes.

WILLIAM. Then make them set fires.

STANLEY. I do that and you will open, not lock, the doors to me?

WILLIAM. Here. The key.

WILLIAM *hands over a key.*

STANLEY. They shall be told to light for an hour a day, any more this gift of weather will count for nothing.

KATHERINE. They need fuel. The woods around are damp. Kindling in short supply.

STANLEY. Forget the woods. It is time we looked under different stones.

KATHERINE. Where?

STANLEY. They will have their fuel.

## 21.

SHELDONS' *house*. STANLEY *stands on the rug.*

STANLEY. Not one person hath stepped through these doors.
I thought them quick to turn a table upon Sheldon.
To seek a moment's sweet revenge.
But it as if he does still roam this hall, a poltergeist guarding, making note of who to haunt.
Well I do not fear you.
As all this proves me true.
Jewellery, gold, linen, so much here gained at others' blood and tears, all simply gathers dust.
No more evident required than this that it cannot be taken with you.
On the Day of Judgement, this offers no negotiate with the Lord our Father.
It is you and him and him alone.

FRANCIS. M-Mr Stanley?

STANLEY. Here.

FRANCIS *enters carrying two axes.*

FRANCIS. I have the-the axes.

STANLEY. Not scared of him still, Francis?

FRANCIS. S-silly, I know.

STANLEY. You are a free man, Francis. Take this rug. Arctic fox, it will keep you warm.

FRANCIS. If you think God would… ap-approve.

STANLEY. I think He would. The axe.

FRANCIS *hands it over.*

Let us hope you sharpened sufficient, Francis.

STANLEY *swings it down on the table. Smashes it. He enjoys it.* FRANCIS *joins in. They continue until they are exhausted.*

## 22.

*High up, the boundary stone. Snow still falls.* WILLIAM *and* JOHN HANCOCK.

HANCOCK. I've walked from point to point: the well, Far Oak and now this stone. 'Tis same at each spot. No supplies. Nothing. All money still there. Weather leaves routes impassable.

WILLIAM. Snow was meant to be our friend.

HANCOCK. Friendship's a bastard, in't it.

WILLIAM. There are tests at every corner.

HANCOCK. If it continues, how long can we survive? What supplies have we left?

*A moment.*

WILLIAM. Look out there, John. It would be so easy, would it not? Into the woods, follow the line, dip low, follow the river, cut up through the rocks, over Curbar Edge. Gone. Not a guard or obstacle to face.

HANCOCK. True.

WILLIAM. Yet we stay. Why? Is it pure faith?

HANCOCK. Plays its part.

WILLIAM. Fear?

*They stare out.*

HANCOCK. Trust, William. Nothing is less noble to break than trust.

*They stare out.*

I have livestock.

WILLIAM. I cannot ask that of you.

HANCOCK. You did not ask. You were given.

## 23.

UNWIN*'s lodgings. A fire burns. Various small animal carcasses hang from the ceiling.*

HARRIET *watches as* UNWIN *butchers a rabbit.*

UNWIN. Living off the land is a right. Should not rely on others to bring food to yer table. Can't hunt it, kill it, gut 'n' skin it then don't expect to eat it. Rabbits are stupid, easiest to start with. First. Tek its belly, squeeze it, get that last bit of piss out. Next, back legs to you. Get yer knife, mek incision, not t' deep, depth can puncture guts. Cut top to bottom. Hands in. Pull out guts. Get 'em all out. Turn it over. Incision in middle of back. Pull skin right off. One way then other. Legs, head, chop off. Give it wash. Chuck in salt water. Easy. What parents never show a child how to butcher?

HARRIET. Weren't even allowed a knife.

UNWIN. Better off with them dead, aren't yer.

HARRIET. I like knives.

UNWIN. Right, your turn.

*A knock at the door.*

Wait.

JOHN HANCOCK *and* WILLIAM *enter.*

Customary to wait.

WILLIAM. Harriet, what brings you here?

HARRIET. Learning to butcher. I have my own knife now.

UNWIN. Taken her under my wing.

HANCOCK. Crow sheltering an adder.

WILLIAM. You're selling meat, Unwin?

UNWIN. As I have done every day since I remember.

WILLIAM. What mark you inflate it to?

UNWIN. This why you're here?

HANCOCK. They are yer neighbours, yer friends.

UNWIN. He asked me to stay, I stayed. Unlike your wife, John. Hence, I provide a service, service that is required. I bait. Trap. Butcher. All that is my work. And yes, in return, I ask a price. Prices they are prepared to pay.

HANCOCK. As they have no other option.

UNWIN. What good is saving coins, cloth, if any moment you may cease? People do not want to die hungry, Reverend. Put the knife down, Harriet.

HARRIET *does*.

The supplies are late again.

WILLIAM. They are.

HANCOCK. See coins in those words.

WILLIAM. Unwin, you have skill. A skill we desperate require.

UNWIN. I should help those who won't help themselves?

WILLIAM. Not won't: can't.

UNWIN. Bollocks. Many are plenty well. Could go out, bait, but they don't. Instead they have you traipsing through snow laying blame at me, a man who creates work, who works for their bone-idle ways. This is the time for endeavour, to build, cut waste.

WILLIAM. People will die.

UNWIN. They're far more resourceful than you think. They want to live, they'll either pay, or, you watch, they'll learn to hunt. Don't pull a face, John, I don't see you helping them.

HANCOCK. I will share my livestock

UNWIN. Guilt can't pay yer wife's debt, John.

WILLIAM. If you die here what will all this coin do you?

UNWIN. I'm not intending to die. This, plague, when it goes, a new future will need to be made. Those that see that now we are the ones who will shape it.

## 24.

*The Delph. Thick, deep, snow.* EMMOTT *watches* ROWLAND *drag several sacks of food.*

EMMOTT. Rowland, must stop doing this, the path is too treacherous. You could slip, fall into the ravine. Yer'd break your neck. Lie there. Unfound. I'd think yer'd forgotten me. Stand here for days, weeks.

ROWLAND. I'd never forget yer.

EMMOTT. Well, yer should. Rowland, I'm tired. So tired. And hungry. And cold. And scared. And angry.

ROWLAND. Let me cross.

EMMOTT. No.

ROWLAND. Let me hold yer.

EMMOTT. No.

ROWLAND. I am stuck, Emmott. All avoid me at home. Let me be with yer.

EMMOTT. No.

ROWLAND. Have more gone?

EMMOTT. Not a single one. Eight more days is all we need. Some bastard, some weak old bastard will ruin it. Spread it again.

ROWLAND. Must stay strong. It is an ask but yer must.

EMMOTT. I want to live, Rowland. I want to live.

ROWLAND. We will grow old by each other's side, our bones will rest together –

EMMOTT *and* ROWLAND. – till they are nought but dust.

EMMOTT. Oh, Rowland, yer do listen.

*Beat.* ROWLAND *throws the bags to* EMMOTT.

### 25.

*Church. The* VILLAGERS *huddle together. Frosted breath fills the air.* WILLIAM *stands before the congregation.*

WILLIAM. Together we prayed for cold.

*The* VILLAGERS *mutter 'aye'.*

Our unity, our common cause in prayer has been rewarded. Proof that our mighty Father listens.

ALL. Amen.

WILLIAM. Outside the snow lies deep. A blanket that smothers. It provides respite. It brings its own dangers. From those you must protect yourself.

EMMOTT. How?

WILLIAM. Light fires. Do not bring more misery into your homes.

JOHN WILSON. Some do not have wood to burn.

WILLIAM. This will be rectified.

MARY COOPER. Others hoard!

UNWIN *is heckled.*

UNWIN. All a bunch of lazy feckless bastards! Want me to wipe yer arses for yer as well!

WILLIAM. Order. Order! Each here needs each other. Now I ask those who are able enough to assist to join me in gathering what we can from the woods. To spread our finds amongst those less able. That way they may still remain your neighbour.

*There is almost a sense of agreement.*

EMMOTT. Hear that, Unwin?

UNWIN. I'm not deaf.

WILLIAM. Twenty-three days since we last lost a life. A true blessing.

ALL. Amen.

ELIZABETH SYDALL. Only five more days to go!

*A ripple of excitement from the* VILLAGERS.

UNWIN. (Thank fuck.)

WILLIAM. Yes, yes, though I fear the snow doesn't kill what we fear most, but keeps it dormant.

JOHN HANCOCK. What are yer saying?

WILLIAM. The snow still falls. It will last longer than five days. I ask you to not have twenty-eight days as your target.

VILLAGERS. What?

EMMOTT. Were the length you set.

WILLIAM. Yes. I ask you to extend faith. We must have clarity. The snow must melt. Then if a week passes, with no more loss of life, we will know for certain it is over.

JOHN HANCOCK. You break yer word, William.

WILLIAM. No, John. No.

JOHN HANCOCK. We have trusted you.

KATHERINE. We never foresaw this.

EMMOTT. Then what, when those seven days pass?

WILLIAM. Let us see it does.

EMMOTT. Change yer mind again? I gave you twenty-eight days, Reverend. I fought for you on that.

UNWIN. If yer need a fix of love, if I have to, I will oblige yer, Emmott.

JOHN WILSON. Watch your mouth.

UNWIN. Alright for you, John, you've got it on tap.

ELIZABETH SYDALL. I cannot have a baby here!

MARY COOPER. It's that sordid cock and womb that's brought plague upon us.

EMMOTT. And not a tailor that a greedy cow took in as lodger!?

KATHERINE. Stop this blame of each other. The fault lies with no individual.

EMMOTT. I know full well. Everyone could find a fault of their own making. That were my point. See already we are on our arses. It pushes how we behave. How long can we live on charity for?

JOHN WILSON. Elizabeth is soon to give birth: how can we provide for our families? We can't work.

UNWIN. Bullshit. Yer love not working!

JOHN HANCOCK. John speaks truth: can't work, no one will buy our lead.

UNWIN. Your wife would say the only miner you've ever been is a shit one, John.

JOHN HANCOCK. Your neck has been overdue a breaking for years, Unwin!

*Red mist has descended for* JOHN HANCOCK. UNWIN *takes cover.*

UNWIN. I'd knock yer out, John Hancock, if I were only allowed to touch yer!

WILLIAM. John, stop!

*In the mêlée* WILLIAM *is knocked over.* KATHERINE *goes over to him.*

UNWIN. He just punched a man of God!

KATHERINE. Enough, Unwin!

JOHN HANCOCK *has stopped, horrified of his actions.* WILLIAM *stands.*

Let us be better than these maddening times we live in.

JOHN HANCOCK. Reverend?

WILLIAM. As Katherine says: we must be dignified despite what we endure.

FRANCIS *approaches.*

FRANCIS. Rev-Reverend –

WILLIAM. What is it, Francis?

FRANCIS. I… I-I c-come fr-from, from, from…

UNWIN. Oh, who made him the messenger? Spit it out, Francis!

FRANCIS. We ha-have… not made it.

*Beat.*

HOWE. Who, Francis?

FRANCIS. I-Isaac Wilson The… mark is, is, is upon him.

WILLIAM. God rest his soul.

ALL. Amen.

HOWE. Did yer touch him, Francis?

FRANCIS. I-I – /

HARRIET. He touched him! (Were he soggy?)

FRANCIS. / that is-is-n-n-

ELIZABETH SYDALL. He is infected!

KATHERINE. We do not know that.

JOHN WILSON. Stay away from Elizabeth!

FRANCIS. M-Mary?

*Beat.*

MARY COOPER. Get out, Francis. Away!

*FRANCIS flees.*

UNWIN (*to* HARRIET). That's that sorted then, we're going.

STANLEY. You will stay where you are. Each one of you.

UNWIN. Will we?

STANLEY. You will. For you have committed. That commitment will be honoured.

HARRIET. Or what?

STANLEY. Or risk the wrath from above. There be greater matters than you and I. Much, much greater.

HARRIET. Bears?

UNWIN. Quiet, Harriet.

STANLEY. There could be no greater sin than failure of your Christian soul. Now go, return to your homes. Those who said they would will come and collect wood. It will be distributed in due course. Look to prayer for support.

*The* VILLAGERS *disperse.* WILLIAM, STANLEY *and* KATHERINE.

Upon its reading, a passage did strike me hard last night: 'Greater love has no one than this, that he lay down his life for his friends.' Good day, Mrs Mompesson. Reverend.

*STANLEY exits.*

## 26.

FRANCIS *runs screaming through the woods, dropping sticks as he does.* HARRIET *is chasing him with a knife.*

HARRIET. Come back, a' only want to take one of yer ears!

> HARRIET *continues to pursue* FRANCIS *into the woods. Shortly after,* EMMOTT, ELIZABETH SYDALL *and* MARY COOPER *enter. They are collecting sticks.*

MARY COOPER. Is yer fancy man alright with yer doing this?

EMMOTT. Even if he weren't, she's had enough years of a man telling her what she can and can't do.

MARY COOPER. She obviously didn't listen closely enough to the bit when he said she couldn't go devouring another man's seed.

ELIZABETH SYDALL. I wish to do my part.

MARY COOPER. Well if yer waters break I ain't getting up in there. Have to walk yerself down.

EMMOTT. She'll be fine. Won't yer, Mother.

ELIZABETH SYDALL. Yes.

> ELIZABETH SYDALL *and* EMMOTT *separate from* MARY COOPER, *as they continue to collect sticks.*

MARY COOPER. Eh, it weren't that bad a fart!

> HARRIET *watches* MARY COOPER *gather a collection of sticks.*

HARRIET. Yer taking Francis's house.

MARY COOPER. Sticks aren't houses.

HARRIET. He's done it real good. Better than my den. I were going to set it on fire. When he were asleep in it.

MARY COOPER. He came to the woods for peace, let him have it.

HARRIET. Nah, you drove him up here and peace, is boring.

> HARRIET *goes.* MARY COOPER *goes to look for* FRANCIS.

MARY COOPER. Francis, Francis?!

KATHERINE *enters carrying sticks.*

EMMOTT. Mrs Mompesson, do not be alone, come join us.

KATHERINE. Thank you.

EMMOTT. That is not worthy of thanks. Carrying, gathering sticks and firewood through snow, for all others, that is worthy of thanks. Now I want Mother to tell me what she will do once this all comes to an end.

KATHERINE. The snow?

EMMOTT. No, this. The plague. When it passes. What is next? You must have many ideas. Leave us bloody riffraff? No, I joke. You will stay. I see that clearly. This is your home now. Why d'yer hesitate?

KATHERINE. I have not thought on it.

EMMOTT. Come now. We have to believe in something, we have to hope, it is essential. Mother?

ELIZABETH SYDALL. I wish to visit a market. To walk between the stalls. To purchase a garment of my own choosing.

EMMOTT. Then we shall do that. Mrs Mompesson?

KATHERINE. We used to visit a beach. Robin Hood's Bay. The children. William and I. It is the time I think of as being most joyous. I wish for us to return to it.

EMMOTT. I have never seen the sea. What is it like?

KATHERINE. It is so vast. It has a language of its own. George, my youngest, he did give me this shell.

KATHERINE *takes a shell out from her pocket. She listens to it.*

With this I forever carry the memory of that moment. Here. Put this to your ear.

EMMOTT *takes the shell from* KATHERINE. *She places it to her ear.*

EMMOTT. What is that?

KATHERINE. That is the sound of the sea.

EMMOTT. The sound is caught in there?

KATHERINE. Nestled, I prefer to say.

EMMOTT *is delighted by what she hears.*

EMMOTT. Hello, sea.

EMMOTT *passes it to* ELIZABETH SYDALL, *who is equally delighted.*

Does that mean sound is forever alive? Echoing throughout eternity? That my voice may reach a place I could never live to see?

KATHERINE. It would be a wonder to believe so.

EMMOTT. I am going to say it does. I am going to say that words will always be out there circling in time, hunting, searching for each other. You should say something to your children. Right now. Go on. I shall do it with Rowland. Rowland Torre, I do love yer! Mother…

*A moment.*

ELIZABETH SYDALL. Goodbye, John Sydall!

EMMOTT *gestures to* KATHERINE. *A moment.*

KATHERINE. Dear hearts, I do miss you. I do love you so deeply. We will be returned together.

EMMOTT. There they go. Out there. Forever.

ELIZABETH SYDALL. She did not get this mind from me.

EMMOTT. Well, it weren't my father, so I think yer do yerself disservice. This is what I want, Mrs Mompesson: I'm going to teach you and my new brother or sister to read. Father can no longer forbid.

KATHERINE. Who taught you to read?

EMMOTT. Stanley.

KATHERINE. Mr Stanley taught you?

EMMOTT. The Bible were our only book but it were taught
with as much care and love of words as if I had a key to
every word ever written and does exist in the entire world.
When Stanley were made leave, Father, if he truly were the
man of God he said he were, should have kept up my
brothers', my sisters' reading, so they too could learn God's
word. But no, he were a man who only wanted God on his
vengeful terms. But by then the gift, to me, were given.
Truth were that gift, seed Stanley planted, were what made
me question, rebel, against everything he had ever spoke.
Mrs Mompesson, the more that can read, can write, the more
can challenge, stand on their own two feet. That's what I
want, when this ends, Rowland and I will share this gift as
wide and far and with as many as we can so that they have
a voice to call their own.

## 27.

*Rectory.* KATHERINE *and* WILLIAM.

KATHERINE. What have I done?! That girl, so bright, she, and
all else here are doomed because of what I have said. A
world she will never see because I dreamt of crows. Birds
which as you said were clear the marker of death. Not life.
Near hundred lives lost to a whim. A need rooted in my own
selfishness!

WILLIAM. Katherine –

KATHERINE. We have nothing to show for it. Our dear
beloved children. I did not endure labour to simply hand
them over. I want to watch them grow, to educate, cherish.
Many moments now will never be. Never. We communicate
through letters, it is not a natural state for any mother.
William. Our dear hearts…

WILLIAM *tries to hold* KATHERINE. *She brushes him
away.*

WILLIAM. They are well, I know it.

KATHERINE. Three weeks without word. Three weeks, William. Every night I wish I'd gone to them. I wish to leave.

STANLEY *enters*.

STANLEY. I have intruded.

WILLIAM. No, Mr Stanley, enter.

STANLEY *nods*.

STANLEY. Isaac Wilson is buried.

WILLIAM. Eat with us, Thomas.

STANLEY. I do not wish to intrude.

WILLIAM. Please.

KATHERINE. This house rattles with only us here. It is a place for children. Hollow without them.

STANLEY. Anne often said it needed the sound of children's voices.

KATHERINE. Yes.

STANLEY. How old are your children?

WILLIAM. Five and three.

KATHERINE. What of you, Thomas?

STANLEY. Children? It was not part of God's plan for us.

KATHERINE *gestures*. STANLEY *sits*.

We were married a week shy of fifty years. I believe she knew me better than even God. Every moment, every thought. Perhaps I am easy to predict. It is as if she foresaw this. She always had this village's interest in her heart. She insisted I buried her here. No other reason would have brought my return. A final duty. Now the village where she lays swells with loss. This is bigger than we are. Bigger than those within these borders. We cannot lose sight of that.

WILLIAM *looks to* KATHERINE. *She nods*.

**28.**

*Village.* JOHN WILSON, HARRIET *and* UNWIN.

UNWIN. Harriet Stubbs is a miracle! The girl is immune.

JOHN WILSON. Immune?

UNWIN. Are not her entire family deceased?

JOHN WILSON. They are.

UNWIN. Yet she lives. For one reason, one reason only. This.

UNWIN *produces a bottle.*

HARRIET. I drank it. They didn't. They're dead.

UNWIN. Her own words. Her own living testament. John after all these years. Finally, Elizabeth. Wife-to-be. Father. They look to you, to provide. The provision she looks for is life.

JOHN WILSON. We have prayer –

UNWIN. Yes, prayer, prayer is a vital tool. A must. Without prayer this remedy's power is defunct. Tell them how yer prayed.

HARRIET. To God.

UNWIN. With her full heart and her soul she prayed to God.

JOHN WILSON. What is in it?

UNWIN. The rarest, most precious herbs.

JOHN WILSON. How were it discovered?

HARRIET. I put it in a pot.

UNWIN. She were guided every step by the gracious hand of our Lord. Here. Put that under your nose.

JOHN WILSON. It is –

UNWIN. Vile, yes! Like the plague itself! To attack the devil must fight as if a devil yerself. Now, we have limited supply. We come to you first as your family deserve the chance of life ahead of all others. For you are pure souls.

JOHN WILSON. What do you want for it?

UNWIN. What do you have?

JOHN WILSON. This is the remedy that saved your life?

UNWIN. She is stood before you. She walks from grave to grave untouched.

HARRIET. If Mother had drank this she would not be dead.

UNWIN. Yes!

HARRIET. None will be dead if they drink this.

UNWIN. Yes!

JOHN WILSON. This is all I have.

UNWIN. Then that is all we need.

*They exchange.*

Here, John. Go forth. Save yer family.

JOHN WILSON. God bless you both.

UNWIN. No, God bless you, John Wilson.

JOHN WILSON *goes.*

HARRIET. I pissed in that one.

UNWIN. As yer should. I always thought well of him. Must have commit some serious sin for the fear of death does turn him weak.

HARRIET. If they all die they'll be upset with us?

UNWIN. If so they'll have to take it up with us in heaven. And if they live they will forever sing our praises.

MARY COOPER *races on. A complete panic.*

MARY COOPER. Where is the reverend?

UNWIN. Who is dead now?

MARY COOPER. No, it's Elizabeth Sydall, her bastard's on the way!

**29.**

*A cry of agony.* ELIZABETH SYDALL *is in labour.*

WILLIAM. Dear Father, oh merciful, heavenly Father, I pray, do not take this child. Let there be a ray for all to cling to. Show us out of the darkness there can be light. That life can thrive in face of such adversity.

KATHERINE *approaches.*

KATHERINE. A boy.

*A baby cries.*

He listens, William, he listens! Life!

*Bright-blue sky. Church. Wedding of* ELIZABETH SYDALL *and* JOHN WILSON. VILLAGERS *lay flowers. A path is created.* ELIZABETH SYDALL *and* JOHN WILSON *walk along this path, carrying their baby. The* VILLAGERS *dance and sing.*

EMMOTT. If ever two were one, then surely we.
   If ever man were loved by wife, then thee.
   If ever wife was happy in a man,
   Compare with me, ye women, if you can.
   I prize thy love more than whole mines of gold,
   Or all the riches that the East doth hold.
   My love is such that rivers cannot quench,
   Nor ought but love from thee give recompense.
   Thy love is such I can no way repay;
   The heavens reward thee manifold, I pray.
   Then while we live, in love let's so persevere,
   That when we live no more, we may live ever.

*Crows cry.* EMMOTT *collapses.*

**30.**

EMMOTT. Keep away!

SYDALLS' *cottage*. EMMOTT *lies gravely ill.*
ELIZABETH SYDALL *and* JOHN WILSON *by her
bedside.*

Mother…!

ELIZABETH SYDALL. Hush now.

EMMOTT. Away… Tell Rowland how I love him.

ELIZABETH SYDALL. I shall, I promise. Rest now, child.

JOHN WILSON. Fresh water. Apply to her skin. It will provide
some comfort.

EMMOTT. Do not touch me. Out.

ELIZABETH SYDALL. Emmott.

EMMOTT. OUT. OUT!!

EMMOTT *screams at her mother. She vomits.*

ELIZABETH SYDALL. The bucket.

JOHN WILSON *brings it over.*

JOHN WILSON. Here.

EMMOTT. …Must not touch me… finally the two of you…

ELIZABETH SYDALL. We will not leave you.

EMMOTT. You must. Go. Go. Both of you. Close the door.
Seal it. Go…

JOHN WILSON *drags* ELIZABETH SYDALL *out.*

Rowland…

*The Delph.*

ROWLAND. I am here!

EMMOTT. Shall lie together. Our bones entwined till dust…
Rowland…

ROWLAND *waits.*

ROWLAND. Do yer hear me, Emmott?

ROWLAND *waits*.

EMMOTT....Rowland...

ROWLAND. Emmott?

    EMMOTT *dies*. ROWLAND *waits*.

    Still here.

    ROWLAND *waits*.

    Always here. Always.

    EMMOTT *is carried away by the crows*.

## 31.

HOWE, ELIZABETH SYDALL (*babe in arms*), JOHN WILSON, KATHERINE, WILLIAM *and* STANLEY *all stand over* EMMOTT'*s grave*. ROWLAND *continues to wait. Crows become silent just as* HOWE *finishes covering* EMMOTT'*s grave*.

HOWE. Done.

    *He makes another mark on his shovel. A moment.*

    I must keep count.

KATHERINE. At least wait.

ELIZABETH SYDALL. What were my daughter?

HOWE. Which one? Emily I know she were fifth because I remember making the first cross through her. Ellen were nineteen. Alice were a bit later –

WILLIAM. Quiet now, Howe.

HOWE. Wish to know your sons? Your first husband?

WILLIAM. She asks about Emmott.

STANLEY. Seventy-fourth.

HOWE. Could be seventy-five if Humphrey Merrell is included cos it may have been the cold that took him.

STANLEY. Seventy-fourth.

HOWE. She were the seventy-fourth.

STANLEY. You have more to attend.

HOWE. Plenty.

STANLEY. Then attend.

> HOWE *nods and goes.* ELIZABETH SYDALL *and* JOHN WILSON *go to leave.* ELIZABETH SYDALL *stops and returns.*

ELIZABETH SYDALL. It is not a guest, it has keys to every door. Returns to houses thought seen enough.

WILLIAM. Place your faith in God.

ELIZABETH SYDALL. Because he lets me live? Is that what his faith is? Life? This life?

JOHN WILSON. Come, Elizabeth, let us go.

> ELIZABETH SYDALL *and* JOHN WILSON *go.*

WILLIAM. All I offer are the same words.

STANLEY. The words are true.

KATHERINE. They are raw.

> MARY COOPER *approaches.*

MARY COOPER. Reverend. All the Naylors are dead. Four of them huddled together in their bed.

> WILLIAM *stares blankly.*

Reverend, this is not the time for you to take a vow of silence.

STANLEY. Send for Howe.

> MARY COOPER *goes.*

**32.**

*Rectory.* KATHERINE *and* WILLIAM. KATHERINE *is
reading a letter.*

KATHERINE. 'What spirit! What verve! What faith! Words
forever be inadequate in face of such service. No patron has
e'er been so served. You prove me a wise man. There is not
a man in the land who has said differ. Oh you shalt have your
pick of whatever parish you do desire, William' –

WILLIAM. That man, Saville, sits on his arse, drinking wine,
revelling in glory, as if he himself, not Eyam's people, be
responsible for the sickness not running rife through his
allies' estates. The smugness permeates, despite around us,
death, death, death. It is misery, his salvation is our misery.
Well, fuck him!

KATHERINE. Now you truly are a local.

WILLIAM. What is a local? On arrival I thought they were a
wild, half-bred folk, who looked like they had yet to have
daylight introduced upon them. People I wanted, could learn,
nothing from, that were beneath me. I were that wrong. That
shallow. That judgemental.

KATHERINE. They did not make it easy, William.

WILLIAM. The baggage was mine not theirs. It was pure
vanity. And so I led them to their own death. Local, I am not
worthy of such a title.

KATHERINE. Just as well, they shalt never give it you.

WILLIAM. Did I embark upon this quarantine for noble
reasons, Katherine? Is the truth more vicious: that it were my
deepest wish to be celebrated. Praised. From country house
to country house.

KATHERINE. That is not the reason. It never did come into
your thinking.

WILLIAM. Did it not?

KATHERINE. William, no.

WILLIAM. It rages. This storm we ride. It grows and grows,
darker and darker, we know not if this is its nadir, or if there
is still further to plummet.

KATHERINE. William, the plague is not our master.

WILLIAM. Katherine, that is the very truth. We cannot, we must not cower to it, none here ever wish to be thought of as victim. We will not wait upon *it* any longer.

*And as if in the same thought we now at...*

## 33.

*The Delph. A service. The* VILLAGERS *spread thinly across the hill.* WILLIAM *stands before them.*

WILLIAM. Today we strike back.
    We ride the storm.
    Not let it shift and shape us.
    Here, at this spot, we will meet.
    Here I will lead you in praise.
    Across these banks, through the trees.
    Nature will be our church.
    Still unified we will support one another but stifling the proximity on which it feeds.
    If death reaches within your door, those who still inhabit mark it with a cross.
    Be proud as you do.
    Show to all the mark of our Lord.
    Show that, like Jesus himself, a sacrifice was made for the greater good.
    The graveyard is full, bodies will not lay upon bodies.
    Upon your land you will bury those who our merciful Lord does take.
    So that forever they lie as close to you in death as they did in life.
    It is an honour to look along these banks.
    You give me strength.
    You have shown me the society I wished lead.
    Never could a man be so blessed.
    Now let us pray.

KATHERINE *stands by* WILLIAM. STANLEY *looks at*
WILLIAM. *At the* VILLAGERS *who have followed his
words. He tilts his head in prayer.*

## 34.

HANCOCKS'*farm. The sun scorches the earth.* JOHN
HANCOCK *watches on as* MARY TALBOT *digs a grave.*

JOHN HANCOCK. If not the plague, it'll be the digging that
    kills you. Two graves now dug. Yer barely break the surface,
    Mary. Foxes, crows, they will be scratching at them.

MARY TALBOT. Nothing can be done.

JOHN HANCOCK. It can.

MARY TALBOT. Stay where you are, John.

JOHN HANCOCK. Foxes, crows.

MARY TALBOT. I heard.

JOHN HANCOCK. They eat everything. Not an inch spared.
    Eyes. They eat eyes.

MARY TALBOT. I know full well what they do, John. It
    changes nothing. Yer would not ask me to make the sacrifice
    you think to make.

JOHN HANCOCK. Perhaps, like Howe, I am immune.

MARY TALBOT. Cannot take that chance. If I fall, leave Howe
    to the task.

JOHN HANCOCK. He will take all you have left as his charge.

MARY TALBOT. It won't get him far.

    MARY TALBOT *continues to dig.*

    WILLIAM *approaches.*

WILLIAM. I bring supplies.

JOHN HANCOCK. Look to Mary's farm. She digs a grave, William.

WILLIAM. Not another?

JOHN HANCOCK. To follow your instruction, I must watch, watch my friend bury her own child? The second in as many days.

WILLIAM. Yes.

JOHN HANCOCK. You hear your words?

WILLIAM. I do, John.

JOHN HANCOCK. Ask us to deny our most basic of instinct.

WILLIAM. Feel no shame, the weight fall upon me not you.

JOHN HANCOCK. Do not ask this of me.

WILLIAM. You shall take heed of my instruction. I will not have you added to that weight. You understand, John. Do you?

JOHN HANCOCK. She has no help.

WILLIAM. Then that is my duty. Mine. John, mine. I will pay visit. Assist.

JOHN HANCOCK. Dig her grave?

WILLIAM. If that is the comfort I can offer.

JOHN HANCOCK. You ask all to stay within, to not assist. Then walk from door to door calling on all. Think it is maybe you should curb yer visits, William?

WILLIAM. You do not mean that, John Hancock.

JOHN HANCOCK. I think I know exactly what I mean.

MARY TALBOT *continues to dig*.

**35.**

*Churchyard.* MARY COOPER *stares at* EDWARD*'s grave.*
HOWE *whistles cheerfully as he drags a covered body towards
an open grave.*

MARY COOPER. Must yer whistle?

HOWE. Makes the load that bit lighter.

MARY COOPER. Please.

HOWE. That is a foreign word from your mouth, Mary.

> HOWE *watches* MARY COOPER, *he stops whistling.*
> HOWE *starts to haul the body. It hits a rock. He tugs at it
> but it won't come free.*

> No thought of helping me? Nothing to fear, Mary, appears
> we're both blessed with immunity.

MARY COOPER. Pray I was not, I pray it was I that were took.

HOWE. There's plenty who'd swap that prayer with you.

> HOWE *yanks the body till it's free.*

MARY COOPER. Howe.

HOWE. Fear not, I showed your Edward more respect. Dug
him a good hole.

MARY COOPER. Nice plot you gave him.

HOWE. He weren't too bad a boy, your Edward.

MARY COOPER. That really Unwin?

HOWE. Indeed.

MARY COOPER. It is not only the gentle he takes.

HOWE. Aye. Finally it is the wicked's turn.

> HOWE *is by the grave.*

> Christ, won't need to cover him, he stank alive, but now,
> Jesus, even flies won't touch him in this state.

> HOWE *rolls* UNWIN *into the grave.*

MARY COOPER. That's it?

HOWE. I normally offer a little prayer at this stage. Not today though. Never saw this, did yer, Unwin, me dragging yer to a lonely grave. Serves yer right for being a shite-hawk seeking profit in misery. Not even yer own little pet shadow here to wish yer goodbye. Tell yer, this is no civil duty – this will cost yer. I will be visiting yer house, all that coin, cloth yer reaped, that will be my payment. All f' nowt. What d'yer say, Mary? Fancy a little stroll round to Unwin's, load up on trinkets?

MARY COOPER. I knew all along it were your way.

HOWE. Yes or no?

MARY COOPER. He did mock my Edward.

HOWE. Aye, he did.

> HOWE *starts to shovel the earth into the grave.*

Simple layer will do for now.

> *A groan.*

Feed that stomach of yours, Mary.

MARY COOPER. It is not me, it is something other.

> *Another groan. Louder.* HOWE *looks into the grave. Another louder groan.* MARY COOPER *approaches.*

It cannot be.

HOWE. The dead walk!

> HOWE *jumps into the grave with his shovel, he hits the body. Screams of pain.*

UNWIN....Help...

HOWE. Get you gone, devil!

> HOWE *goes to strike again.* MARY COOPER *stops him.*

MARY COOPER. What if he were never dead?

HOWE. Cannot be.

MARY COOPER. Did yer not check?

HOWE. Outside of his house were marked with the cross.

MARY COOPER. Get him out.

> HOWE *drags* UNWIN *up.* UNWIN *lies on the ground.*

Sure he is not dead?

HOWE. How can I know?

> HOWE *considers. Kicks* UNWIN. *A yelp. Kicks him again.*

MARY COOPER. He already screamed.

> *Kicks him again.*

HOWE. Very well, he's alive. Unwin?

UNWIN. You… you… you saved me!

HOWE. Aye, I did just that.

MARY COOPER. We thought yer dead.

UNWIN. I remember a cough. Harriet did provide a remedy. Then I fell into a deep sleep.

HOWE. Remedy?! There I think is our answer. She poisoned yer.

UNWIN. Poison? But she…

MARY COOPER. The girl is a ghoul. I've seen her sniffing round these graves.

UNWIN. My head is bleeding.

HOWE. Let's not dwell on that. You be a miracle.

UNWIN. Is it so?

HOWE. Oh aye. Come, let's get yer warm.

> *They help* UNWIN *away.*

> *Song. Crows circle.*

**36.**

MARY TALBOT *digs her own grave.* JOHN HANCOCK *watches.*

*She stops.*

MARY TALBOT. My name is Mary Talbot. This is the land our heavenly Father did bestow upon me. My husband I buried here. My children I bury here. I will now rest here. And I will rest well, for this land I take to my grave.

MARY TALBOT *collapses.* JOHN HANCOCK *walks towards her and lifts her into her grave.*

**37.**

*Village.* WILLIAM *and* STANLEY. FRANCIS *approaches, ravished with the plague.*

STANLEY. Francis?

FRANCIS. Pl-please. I don-don't want to die in the w-woods. Can I-I die here? I want to die in, in, Eyam.

STANLEY. Francis, come.

*He starts to walk closer, but doesn't make it as far as he hoped.* STANLEY *attends him.*

FRANCIS. I could ha-have-have fled.

STANLEY. But you followed the light.

FRANCIS. Let all k-know I co-could have… fled.

STANLEY. Rest now.

FRANCIS. That I-I-I st-stayed. When Sh-Sheldon fled… I stayed…

STANLEY *nods.* WILLIAM *reads the last rites to* FRANCIS. STANLEY *watches on.*

WILLIAM. Unto God's gracious mercy and protection we commit thee. The Lord bless thee and keep thee. The Lord make His face to shine upon thee, and be gracious unto thee. The Lord lift up His countenance upon thee, and give thee peace, both now and evermore. Amen.

STANLEY. Amen.

*Song ends.*

WILLIAM *watches* STANLEY.

I made Anne a promise that I would see this village return to what it were.
This is not what it was.
Nor will it ever be.
Yet I know she will rest forever in peace.
As what I see here is the most shining light;
men, women, children continue to depart in utmost dignity.
Not a single one would I not be proud to lay beside.
The finest company she does keep,
alongside these bravest souls.
So sleep now my dearest Anne, sleep.

WILLIAM. Amen.

*Crows watch on as...*

**38.**

*Village.* HOWE *and* UNWIN *are digging a grave.* HOWE *has a new shovel. They whistle. They harmonise.* ELIZABETH SYDALL, *babe in arms, watches on.*

UNWIN. That shovel new?

HOWE. It is.

*They keep digging.*

UNWIN. Does it matter how deep I dig?

HOWE. Don't tire yerself. Plenty more to be dug.

*They keep digging.*

UNWIN. Were yer wife's the deepest yer dug?

*They keep digging.*

HOWE. It were.

*They keep digging.*

UNWIN. She still watching?

HOWE. She is.

UNWIN. She has no luck, does she? After all these years pining for each other. Reckon I should have a word?

HOWE. No.

UNWIN. Third time's a charm.

HOWE. No.

UNWIN. I can't be a bachelor forever.

UNWIN *approaches* ELIZABETH SYDALL.

Elizabeth –

ELIZABETH SYDALL *screams in* UNWIN*'s face. Years of pain and sadness. Eventually she stops. Collapses.* UNWIN *returns to* HOWE.

Have had worse rejections.

HOWE. Just dig. Dig.

*They continue digging.* HARRIET *approaches.*

HARRIET. Who's that for? Is it for her? Is it for you?

UNWIN. Enough.

HARRIET. Oh no, not yer other husband.

HOWE. This hole will be for you if yer not quiet.

UNWIN *keeps digging.*

HARRIET. I liked yer wedding. I danced. You should marry him next. Or him. His wife's dead.

UNWIN. Enough.

ELIZABETH SYDALL *goes.*

HARRIET. Bye.

UNWIN *gets out of the hole.* HARRIET *backs off.*

Are yer angry with me? Is it because of what I gave yer to drink?

UNWIN *turns away, goes back to the hole.*

UNWIN. Walk away, Harriet.

HARRIET. I did. Went to Tideswell. Got recognised though. Chased away. Lived in woods for a week. Were cold at night. Ate some mushrooms, made me sick out of my arse. It's sore.

UNWIN. Told yer not to eat mushrooms.

HARRIET. I forgot. Won't again. I made new remedy.

UNWIN. Pour it away.

HARRIET. Cow mess. Leaves. Stream water. Bit of bark. We can sell it together.

UNWIN. No. I'm happy here.

HARRIET. In a hole? Did yer die? Were it warm? Did yer see God? That why yer came back? He didn't like yer did he? Would make sense.

UNWIN. I didn't die.

HARRIET. Shoulda done. I put a lot of horrid things in yer drink.

UNWIN. Go now, Harriet.

HARRIET. Where?

HARRIET *waits.*

Nobody will buy it from me without you.

UNWIN. No.

HARRIET. I might try Grindleford. Nobody knows me there.

UNWIN. I'd stay in the woods, Harriet.

HARRIET *goes.*

HOWE. They don't bury themselves, the dead.

HOWE *and* UNWIN *drag a body to the grave. It is* JOHN WILSON...

**39.**

*Churchyard.* WILLIAM *enters waving a burning torch at the circling crows.*

WILLIAM. Away. Away!

KATHERINE *approaches.*

KATHERINE. Intend to stand there fighting crows all day?

WILLIAM. Gone are the days when they simply hovered.

KATHERINE. Your face burns, have you been in the sun all morn?

WILLIAM. Graves lie open. They must be deterred.

KATHERINE. Come, sit in the shade.

WILLIAM. Look how bloated they have become! Will you be the one that pecks at me?

*Concerned,* KATHERINE *watches* WILLIAM *as he approaches, challenging, the crows.*

KATHERINE. William?

WILLIAM. You want my eyes, my soul? Peck me then, go on –

STANLEY *approaches.*

Ah, Thomas! Good day! Tell me, how old is this church?

STANLEY. Over four hundred years.

WILLIAM. Four hundred years! We build these buildings in utter faith, utter faith that people will always need us. But what about when this plague leaves none left? This building will disappear, wrapped away in ivy and leaves. Not even a memory to those left. London has burnt to the ground. Fire it is said halts the plague. God send us a method!

STANLEY. Fire halted the spread?

WILLIAM *nods.*

WILLIAM. They say so.

WILLIAM *sets paper alight. Watches it burn. Drops it on the floor. They watch the fire begin to spread.*

KATHERINE. William? Thomas?

*They watch it burn.*

WILLIAM. It is the cure.

KATHERINE *stamps out the fire.*

KATHERINE. Foolish men. When this storm passes people need foundations to build from. And this storm will pass. Must believe that.

WILLIAM. No. It…

WILLIAM *coughs.*

KATHERINE. William?

WILLIAM *coughs.*

William?

WILLIAM. It is upon me.

WILLIAM *collapses.*

## 40.

KATHERINE. Before the shivers, fevers, boils and all that strip the body of its strength, it is said the air goes sweet.
A gift, memories of days in meadows, of season full in bloom.
To know in advance I imagine render thee calm.
Appreciate all the wonder one has been bestowed.
Children…
Husband…
Love…
I watch him, the man I love, as fever grips, distorting him beyond the shape I've known him forever fit.
And I know, I know he never got that chance.
For the calmness.
For the warmth it would bring.
What is fair of that who offers so much to you, O Lord?

*The* VILLAGERS *gather. They sing a hymn.*

Lord, do not take this man, do not take him from us, I beg.
Hear, outside they gather for him, a man they once would not
even share a simple word, and they sing, they sing for him.
Let him live.
To take him, what hope for them?
If it must be a life then I implore you take that of mine.
And I will come to you full of joy, not regret, but joy.

WILLIAM. Katherine...?

*Rectory. Daytime.* WILLIAM *is in bed.*

KATHERINE. Oh William, I thought you gone... The Lord has
been merciful.

WILLIAM....How long have I lain in this state?

KATHERINE. Three days.

WILLIAM. You were with me for all that time?

KATHERINE. Do not be angry with me.

WILLIAM. I thought I'd never see your face again.

KATHERINE. I am here. William, there is respite. From nine
dear souls departing upon a day, it drops, to two, then one
yesterday, and as yet none today.

WILLIAM. Praise God. The children?

KATHERINE. You will see them. It is what God wishes. Come
now, up, let you see the world.

*They walk. Sun shines. Birds sing.*

It is time we talked of what lies ahead, not lose ourselves in
memories. So here is my opening offer. Warwickshire.

WILLIAM. Warwickshire?

KATHERINE. Somewhere flat, upon a river. An avon. Does Sir
Saville have an avon, amongst his parishes?

WILLIAM. It does sound rather safe. We are not to stay?

KATHERINE. Is that what you would wish?

WILLIAM. Could anyone ever understand what has been experienced here? It does have a river within view.

KATHERINE. I think your eyes do trick you.

WILLIAM. The Derwent. At the bottom of the edge. Must close your eyes very tight. Try. Harder.

KATHERINE. You kid me? It does have trees I suppose.

WILLIAM. And sheep.

KATHERINE. Yes, lots of sheep.

*They stare out.*

WILLIAM. I do love you, Katherine.

*She takes his hand.*

KATHERINE. The air does smell so sweet this evening.

WILLIAM....Katherine..

KATHERINE. There is no blossom.

WILLIAM *shakes his head.*

Let me look for the river again.

WILLIAM *takes* KATHERINE*'s hand.*

At the foot of the edge?

WILLIAM. Yes.

KATHERINE. Now, I do see it.

*They stare out.*

I am ready. I will go inside now.

WILLIAM *keeps hold of her hand.*

Pray with me.

WILLIAM. Very well… O Saviour of the world, who by thy Cross and precious Blood hast redeemed us: save us, and help us, we humbly beseech thee, O Lord /

*The* VILLAGERS *sing. A crow appears.* KATHERINE *slowly walks to it. She offers her hand. The crow takes it.*

/ The Almighty Lord, who is a most strong tower to all them
that put their trust in him, to whom all things in heaven, in
earth, and under the earth, do bow and obey, be now and
evermore thy defence; and make thee know and feel, that there
is none other name under heaven given to man, in whom, and
through whom, thou mayest receive health and salvation, but
only the name of our Lord Jesus Christ... Amen...

KATHERINE *is gone.*

*Silence.*

Katherine?

*And for the first time he is alone.*

### 41.

WILLIAM. Thirteen months after Eyam did first batten its
    hatches the storm did break.
    Katherine fell not short of a month before it did end.
    She were so close.
    So very close.
    There were no life that had not been touched by tragedy.
    The day it passed we took our cloth, our linen: all that could
    carry the seed.
    And burnt them, burnt them to the ground.
    Lit the sky up.
    Lit it up, so all could see what sacrifice befell upon this land.

    *Torches begin to burn.*

    All told, eighty-three of three hundred and fifty-six of
    Eyam's populate did survive.
    Two hundred and seventy-three souls did depart.
    They must not be written from history.
    They must not be forgotten.
    They will be remembered:

    Elizabeth Abell. Mary Abell. William Abell.
    Joseph Alleyn. Margaret Alleyn. Thomas Alleyn. Alleyn
    (infant unnamed).

Abel Archdale.

George Ashe. Godfrey Ashe. Thomas Ashe. Peter Ashe.

Joan Ashmore. Thomas Ashmore.

Margaret Banes. Martha Banes. Mary Banes. Matthew Banes.

Edward Barnsley.

Anne Blackwell. Anthony Blackwell. Anthony Blackwell.
Joan Blackwell. Margaret Blackwell. Sarah Blackwell.

Thomas Bilston.

Alice Bockinge. Edyth Bockinge. Francis Bockinge. Mary
Bockinge. Richard Bockinge. Robert Bockinge. Thomas
Bockinge.

George Butterworth.

Elizabeth Buxton. John Buxton. Margaret Buxton. Mary
Buxton. Robert Buxton.

Anne Chapman. Lydia Chapman. Samuel Chapman.

Ellen Charlesworth.

Edward Cooper. Jonathan Cooper.

Alice Coyle. Anne Coyle. Richard Coyle.

Elizabeth Danyell. John Danyell. Randoll Danyell.

George Darbye. Mary Darbye.

Joan French. Robert French.

Anne Fryth. Elizabeth Fryth. Elizabeth Fryth. Elizabeth
Fryth. Frances Fryth. Francis Fryth. George Fryth. Henry
Fryth. Thomas Fryth. Thomas Fryth. Fryth (infant unnamed).

Anne Glover. Elizabeth Glover.

Margaret Gregory.

Anne Grundy.

Alexander Hadfield. John Hadfield. Robert Hadfield. Samuel
Hadfield.

Anne Hall. Peter Hall. Peter Hall. Samuel Hall.

Alice Hancock. Anne Hancock. Elizabeth Hancock Jr. John
Hancock Jr. John Hancock. Oner Hancock. William
Hancock.

Adam Hawksworth. Alice Hawksworth. Anne Hawksworth.
Francis Hawksworth. Humphrey Hawksworth. Peter
Hawksworth. William Hawksworth. William Hawksworth.

Emmott Heald. Elizabeth Heald. Mary Heald. Thomas Heald.

Thomas Healley.

Joan Howe. William Howe.

Elizabeth Kempe. Lydia Kempe. Michael Kempe. Thomas
Kempe. Robert Kempe.

Anne Lowe. Ellenor Lowe. Elizabeth Lowe. Sarah Lowe.
William Lowe.
Mary Mellor.
Humphrey Merrell.
Katherine Mompesson.
Abraham Morten. Abraham Morten. Anne Morten. Benjamin
Morten. Elizabeth Morten. Francis Morten. Francis Morten.
Grace Morten. Grace Morten. Joseph Morten. Margaret
Morten. Mary Morten. Peter Morten. Rebecca Morten. Ruth
Morten. Sarah Morten. Susanna Morten. William Morten.
Morten (infant unnamed).
Thomas Moseley.
James Mower. Rowland Mower. Rowland Mower Jr.
Anne Naylor. Jonathon Naylor.
Briggett Naylour. Jane Naylour. Joan Naylour.
Jane Nealour. John Nealour. Mary Nealour.
Anne Parsley. Jonas Parsley.
Margaret Percival. Mary Percival. William Percival.
Alice Ragge. Francis Ragge. George Ragge. Thomas Ragge.
Jonathan Ragge
John Rowbottam. Robert Rowbottam. Samuel Rowbottam.
William Rowbottam.
Mary Rowe. William Rowe. Rowe (infant unnamed)
Abel Rowland. Anne Rowland. Hannah Rowland. Mary
Rowland. Thomas Rowland.
Agnes Sheldon.
George Short.
Anne Skidmore. Anthony Skidmore. Mary Skidmore.
Anne Stubbs. Hugh Stubbs. John Stubbs.
Elizabeth Swann. John Swann
Abraham Swinnerton. Anne Swinnerton. Margaret
Swinnerton.
Alice Sydall. Elizabeth Sydall. Ellen Sydall. Emmott Sydall.
John Sydall. Richard Sydall. Sarah Sydall.
Anne Talbot. Bridget Talbot. Briggett Talbott. Jane Talbot.
Joan Talbot. John Talbot. Jonathon Talbot. Katherine Talbot.
Katherine Talbot. Mary Talbot. Richard Talbot. Ruth Talbot.
Robert Talbot.
Alice Taylor. Alice Taylor. James Taylor. Margaret Taylor.
Alice Thornley. Anne Thornley. Edward Thornley.
Elizabeth Thornley. Elizabeth Thornley. Francis Thornley.

Isaac Thornley. John Thornley. Jonathan Thornley. Mary
Thornley. William Thornley.

Alice Thorpe. Elizabeth Thorpe. Elizabeth Thorpe. Mary
Thorpe. Mary Thorpe. Richard Thorpe. Robert Thorpe.
Robert Thorpe. Thomas Thorpe. Thomas Thorpe. Thomas
Thorpe. William Thorpe. William Thorpe.

Amy Torre. Edyth Torre. Godfrey Torre. Humphrey Torre.
Humphrey Torre. Robert Torre. Stythe Torre. John Torre.
Thomas Torre. William Torre.

Anne Townend. Anne Townend. Jane Townend. John
Townend. Townend (infant unnamed).

Anne Trickett. John Trickett. Robert Trickett.

George Viccars.

Elizabeth Warrington.

Mary Whiteley. Mary Whiteley. Nicholas Whiteley. Robert
Whiteley Sr. Thurston Whiteley.

Alice Wilson. Anne Wilson. Deborah Wilson. Francis
Wilson. Isaac Wilson. John Wilson. John Wilson. John
Wilson Jr. Thomas Wilson. Sarah Wilson.

Francis Wood. Joan Wood. John Wood. Thomas Wood.
Robert Wood.

Anne Yealott. Deborah Yealott. John Yealott. Mary Yealott.
Samuel Yealott. Sarah Yealott.

*The entire village is now with him. A community.*

*And they sing.*

*Torches fade.*

*End.*

**www.nickhernbooks.co.uk**

facebook.com/nickhernbooks

twitter.com/nickhernbooks